COMPLETE POEMS
A. E. HOUSMAN

———————◆———————

CENTENNIAL EDITION

COMPLETE POEMS

A. E. HOUSMAN

CENTENNIAL EDITION

with an Introduction by Basil Davenport and
a History of the Text by Tom Burns Haber,
Ohio State University

Henry Holt and Company · New York

A SHROPSHIRE LAD
Authorised Edition
Henry Holt and Company, Inc., 1924

LAST POEMS
Copyright, 1922, by Henry Holt and Company, Inc.
Copyright, 1950, by Barclays Bank, Ltd.

MORE POEMS
Copyright, 1936, by Barclays Bank, Ltd.

COLLECTED POEMS
Copyright, 1940, by Henry Holt and Company, Inc.

The quotation from *The Name and Nature of Poetry* by
A. E. Housman is reprinted by permission of Cambridge
University Press, New York.

CONTENTS

INTRODUCTION

Alfred Edward Housman was born in 1859, one hundred years ago as this goes to press. In 1896, his first book of poems, *A Shropshire Lad,* appeared. It contains sixty-three short poems, all deeply melancholy in mood, all of a chiseled perfection in form, achieving the most exquisite harmonies by the simplest means. In 1922 appeared his *Last Poems,* containing forty-two poems. The total number—of *A Shropshire Lad* and *Last Poems*—which Housman, during his lifetime, selected for publication, a little over a hundred, is almost exactly the same as the *Odes* of Horace. These, too, were deeply melancholy, exquisitely chiseled. There was no progress and no falling-off; indeed, as Housman told us in his Introduction to the *Last Poems,* most of them were written at the same time as the earlier book. There were to be posthumous poems, but during his lifetime that was all.

Nothing else like this has occurred in the history of literature. Twice, a quarter of a century apart, Housman spoke: for all rejected lovers, for young men killed in battle, for those who are homesick for some land of no return, for those to whom the very beauty of earth is a reminder of its evanescence. Once or twice, too, he spoke for those who find it too hard to keep the laws of God and the laws of man, with just a hint of some personal tragedy; for the rest, he was silent.

Or silent at least in poetry. The story is told of Queen Victoria's asking the author of *Alice in Wonderland* for a copy of his next book and receiving a treatise on mathematics. If she had made a similar request of the author of *A Shropshire Lad,* her heirs would have received, in 1903, an edition of the Latin poet Manilius.

The author of some of the most moving verses in the English language was, by profession, a classical scholar, a man of amazing erudition and bristling unapproachability, about whom legends are still told at Cambridge.

He hated women and resented their admission to the university. There is a story, perhaps apocryphal, that at the close of one of his

I

lectures he announced, "My next lecture will be on the Second Satire of Juvenal. As this is one of the obscene satires, I request that the ladies absent themselves from this lecture." At the next lecture, a few daring women students did nevertheless appear; Housman surveyed them and said, "Since I see that there are no ladies present, I will now lecture on the Second Satire of Juvenal."

He did indeed have his lighter side. Once, speaking after dinner in the college hall, he began, "Cambridge has seen strange sights. It has seen Wordsworth drunk, and Porson sober. And now you see me, a better scholar than Wordsworth and a better poet than Porson, neither drunk nor sober, but just betwixt and between."

But what he is primarily remembered for is his personal aloofness and the ferocity of his judgments on the work of fellow scholars. Thus Professor A produced an edition of a Latin author; Professor B reviewed it; Professor Housman remarked that as to such an edition's eliciting such a review, there had been nothing like it since the passage in Milton where Sin gave birth to Death.

His scholarly love of accuracy amounted to a passion. Years ago, I came across an anecdote in the reminiscences of some American book collector, whose name I wish I had noted. When *A Shropshire Lad* first appeared, this collector recognized its importance and obtained a first edition; on the appearance of a second, he wrote to Housman asking if it contained any additions or corrections which would make it desirable from the bibliographic point of view. The usually unapproachable Housman replied (I am quoting from memory):

Dear Sir:
The second edition of my book contains nothing which the first did not, with the exception of a few misprints. I may add that you are the first citizen of your great republic who has ever written to me enclosing an English stamp.
Yours faithfully,
A. E. Housman.

I admire and envy that collector. His coup is the equivalent of landing a very large fish with a very fine line.

The same concern with textual accuracy shows itself in Housman's introductory note to *Last Poems,* which is to me so moving in its reticence that I think it is worth quoting in full. It runs:

Introduction

I publish these poems, few though they are, because it is not likely
that I shall ever be impelled to write much more. I can no longer
expect to be revisited by the continuous excitement under which
in the early months of 1895 I wrote the greater part of my other
book, nor indeed could I well sustain it if it came; and it is best
that what I have written should be printed while I am here to see
it through the press and control its spelling and punctuation.
About a quarter of this matter belongs to the April of the present
year, but most of it to dates between 1895 and 1910.

It is a singular irony that both the posthumous *More Poems* and
the *Additional Poems* in Laurence Housman's memoir should have
appeared, until now, in incorrect texts, with numerous discrepancies
between the English and American editions. For this Centennial Edition, Professor Tom Burns Haber has verified the text, word by word
and letter by letter, from the manuscripts in the Library of Congress.
Nothing would have given Housman greater pleasure than to know
that his poems are at last appearing in an edition as textually correct, down to the last comma, as devoted scholarship can make it.*

Housman's chosen life work was the establishment of a correct text
of Manilius, a minor Latin poet of the Silver Age, who wrote a verse
treatise on the subjects, then not distinguished from each other, of
astronomy and astrology; a treatise which is full of obscurities and has
come down to us full of textual inaccuracies. Early in life, Housman
turned his back on Greek, which he loved, because he could not be
equally great in both languages; and later, in choosing a Latin writer
to whom to devote his life, he considered Propertius, whose poetry he
enjoyed, but rejected him for Manilius, whose poetry (we are told by
one of his memoirists) he scorned, because he considered that the
difficulties with which Manilius abounded would give the greater
opportunity to his particular talent. His edition of Manilius was, he
said, to be his monument.

In looking at this side of Housman's life, one is reminded of a
somewhat similar scholar in fiction, James Blair in Thornton Wilder's
The Cabala. Of him, Wilder wrote:

* *Publisher's Note:* Readers interested in scholarly controversy may
wish to see the *Times Literary Supplement,* London, for April 29,
1955, and July 1, 1955.

Introduction

Thus life stretched . . . bindings . . . bindings . . . catalogues
. . . footnotes. One studied the saints and never thought about
religion. One knew all about Michelangelo and never deeply felt
a single work. . . . The fact is that quite early James Blair had
been frightened by life (in a way which the Princess, in a moment
of misery and inspiration, was to divine later with the cry: What
kind of a stupid mother could he have had?) and had forever after
bent upon books the floodtides of his energy.

Housman's biographers tell us little about his mother, but his
brother, Laurence, in his *A. E. H.,* says:

Alfred was away from home, spending his Easter holiday with old
friends of our mother's, when, on his twelfth birthday, she died
after a long and painful illness. Her death had a profound effect
upon him, for there had been between them a deep bond of af-
fection and understanding. As she neared her end she became
anxious lest his loss of her should affect his attitude to religion;
and when his father wrote to him telling him of her death, there
was something in the nature of a message to that effect. It is
more than likely—though one can only guess—that what they
feared did actually happen; and that his early estrangement from
the religion of his childhood was caused by her death.

A few pages earlier, Laurence Housman has quoted his brother as
himself saying, "I became a deist at thirteen and an atheist at twenty-
one," and the coincidence of dates is surely significant.
I spoke just now of the reticence of Housman's introductory note to
Last Poems. It is interesting to compare that with a passage in his
lecture, *The Name and Nature of Poetry,* delivered in 1933. There
he says:

I think that the production of poetry, in its first stage, is less an
active than a passive and involuntary process; and if I were obliged,
not to define poetry, but to name the class of things to which it
belongs, I should call it a secretion; whether a natural secretion,
like turpentine in the fir, or a morbid secretion, like the pearl in
the oyster. I think that my own case, though I may not deal
with the material so cleverly as the oyster does, is the latter; because I have seldom written poetry unless I was rather out of
health, and the experience, though pleasurable, was generally

4

Introduction

agitating and exhausting. If only that you may know what to avoid, I will give some account of the process.

Having drunk a pint of beer at luncheon—beer is a sedative to the brain, and my afternoons are the least intellectual portion of my life—I would go out for a walk of two or three hours. As I went along, thinking of nothing in particular, only looking at things around me and following the progress of the seasons, there would flow into my mind, with sudden and unaccountable emotion, sometimes a line or two of verse, sometimes a whole stanza at once, accompanied, not preceded, by a vague notion of the poem they were destined to form part of.

He goes on to tell how more of these fragments would occur to him and how, at last, he would have to fit them together and bridge the gaps—"and that was a laborious business," he says of one such bridge that had to be made. "I wrote it thirteen times, and it was more than a twelvemonth before I got it right."

When *The Name and Nature of Poetry* first appeared, I wrote a review of it:

What this deceptively simple recipe for writing a perfect poem leaves out of account is the "continuous state of poetic excitement" (as he said in the introductory note to *Last Poems*) of which he does not speak in his lecture, but which must have been there, boiling constantly under the crust of conscious thought, and ready to break out as soon as consciousness was relaxed. It is singularly characteristic of that synthesis of romantic and classic which is Housman's idiosyncrasy that he would give that excitement its way during the afternoons, the least intellectual part of his life. What he does not tell us is what it was like to live in that state of poetic excitement, which he could not now well sustain, and what caused it. He does not tell us; and he never will.

I am glad of that. I think that the poetry of the romantic revivalists is more thrilling to a schoolboy who reads and understands it in general terms, than to a college student who is furnished with the all too full details which the poets themselves supplied of the domestic difficulties which inspired them. And though we may presume that excitement implies an exciting cause, I am glad we shall never know what the cause was which during a certain time filled the poet's mind with thoughts of hanging and suicide, of soldiers untimely shot and girls unfaithful to their

5

dead sweethearts, and one or two more such themes that he was fain to think of, I believe, rather than of the thing itself. In that respect, at least, it may be said, he is with Shakespeare; no one can read the *Sonnets* or *A Shropshire Lad* without guessing at the tragedy, and no one will ever know what the tragedy was. It is true that as the poet of *A Shropshire Lad* grows older, he grows more indifferent to our knowledge or ignorance; in *A Shropshire Lad* he proudly conceals his wound; in *Last Poems* he still more proudly lets fall a hint or two, in "Hell Gate" and "When the eye of day is shut," for us to do what we like with.

That was written twenty-five years ago, during Housman's lifetime; at that time, I reckoned without the resources of modern biographers. Something more has been discovered about Housman's own tragedy; and that is good, for all knowledge is valuable. But we still do not know why it was that the year 1895, long after the event, should have been the year in which Housman was in a state of continual poetic excitement, and I doubt if he himself could have told us. Some critics have written almost in a tone of moral indignation of Housman's failure to develop, of his writing no differently at the end of his poetic career from what he did at the beginning. But here, surely,

> What's done we partly may compute,
> But know not what's resisted.

No doubt, he could have chosen to edit Propertius instead of Manilius (a change which would have benefited none but professed Latin scholars); but it is very doubtful whether, by simply trying to do so, he could have written more or other than he did, whether he could have prolonged the poetic excitement, and, if he had done so, whether he could have sustained it.

Again, he was certainly an embittered man. Some of his bitterness he turned into poetry—"a morbid secretion, like the pearl in the oyster." Perhaps, as has been implied, he could have prevented himself from becoming embittered; but perhaps, in that case, there would have been no poems. Let us be thankful for what we have.

A word or two should be said as to his technical achievement. He is full of echoes, quotations, even translations—"Sinner's Rue" is an expanded translation of Heine's *"Die Armesuenderblume"*; "Far I hear the bugle blow" is an adaptation of Sarpedon's speech to Glaucus in the *Iliad;* "Epithalamium" contains a translation of Sappho's *"Espere, panta pheron."*

Yet no poet is more individual. One would never take one of his poems for the work of anyone else. His accent can hardly be defined, but one or two characteristics may be pointed out. One is his use of nouns and verbs to do the work that another might have given to adjectives:

> Clay lies still, but blood's a rover;
> Breath's a ware that will not keep.

Akin to this is his use, as adjectives, of participles that still keep a good deal of the force of the verb:

> The year might age, and cloudy
> The lessening day might close,

and

> And I to lift with playing
> From tree and tower and steep
> The light delaying,
> And flute the sun to sleep.

This quatrain also illustrates one of his most characteristic musical devices, the use of one line shorter than the rest. Akin to this is the repetition of the masculine line at the end of the five-line stanza of which he is so fond:

> Bring baskets now, and sally
> Upon the spring's array,
> And bear from hill and valley
> The daffodil away
> That dies on Easter day.

To my ear, those lines have somewhat the effect of the occasional incomplete hexameter in Virgil, a sort of echoing pause—even though it is probable that the Virgilian half-lines are a witness to the fact that Virgil had not finished polishing the *Æneid* when he died. We must remember that Virgil, like Housman, wished his imperfect manuscript to be destroyed.

But Housman himself said in effect, in *The Name and Nature of*

7

Introduction

Poetry, that we cannot explain with any fullness why, of two nearly identical phrases, one should be deeply moving and the other not.

In these six simple words of Milton, "Nymphs and shepherds, dance no more . . . ," what is it that can draw tears, as I know it can, to the eyes of more readers than one? What in the world is there to cry about? Why have the mere words the physical effect of pathos when the sense of the passage is blithe and gay? I can only say, because they are poetry, and find their way to something in man which is obscure and latent, something older than the present organisation of his nature, like the patches of fen which lie here and there in the drained lands of Cambridgeshire.

Housman himself speaks to that something in man. He speaks not only for rejected lovers and bereaved friends, not only for young men dead untimely, but to all who feel the tragic sense of life, to all who feel (even if the feeling is only a mood) that all human alternatives are unhappy.

Horace says,

> *Abstulit clarum cita mors Achillem,*
> *Longa Tithonum minuit senectus—*

("Swift death snatched away Achilles in his glory, Tithonus withered in a long old age")
—and who shall say which fate is the more unhappy? So Housman, who often wrote of the tragedy of early death, wrote also of the tragedy of lingering age:

> And all the years and seasons
> That ever can ensue
> Must now be worse and few.

Whatever causes the tragic mood, we have all felt it and to this mood, Housman speaks, telling us, "Be still, my soul, be still," reminding us that "The Spartans on the sea-wet rock sat down and combed their hair." Stoicism is not, in my belief, the greatest of philosophies, but it is a noble one; and in the works of Housman, it finds fittingly noble expression.

BASIL DAVENPORT

New York City
January 6, 1959

8

A SHROPSHIRE LAD

I

1887

From Clee to heaven the beacon burns,
    The shires have seen it plain,
From north and south the sign returns
    And beacons burn again.

Look left, look right, the hills are bright,
    The dales are light between,
Because 'tis fifty years to-night
    That God has saved the Queen.

Now, when the flame they watch not towers
    About the soil they trod,
Lads, we'll remember friends of ours
    Who shared the work with God.

To skies that knit their heartstrings right,
    To fields that bred them brave,
The saviours come not home to-night:
    Themselves they could not save.

It dawns in Asia, tombstones show
    And Shropshire names are read;
And the Nile spills his overflow
    Beside the Severn's dead.

9

We pledge in peace by farm and town
 The Queen they served in war,
And fire the beacons up and down
 The land they perished for.

'God save the Queen' we living sing,
 From height to height 'tis heard;
And with the rest your voices ring,
 Lads of the Fifty-third.

Oh, God will save her, fear you not:
 Be you the men you've been,
Get you the sons your fathers got,
 And God will save the Queen.

11

Loveliest of trees, the cherry now
Is hung with bloom along the bough,
And stands about the woodland ride
Wearing white for Eastertide.

Now, of my threescore years and ten,
Twenty will not come again,
And take from seventy springs a score,
It only leaves me fifty more.

And since to look at things in bloom
Fifty springs are little room,
About the woodlands I will go
To see the cherry hung with snow.

III

THE RECRUIT

Leave your home behind, lad,
  And reach your friends your hand,
And go, and luck go with you
  While Ludlow tower shall stand.

Oh, come you home of Sunday
  When Ludlow streets are still
And Ludlow bells are calling
  To farm and lane and mill,

Or come you home of Monday
  When Ludlow market hums
And Ludlow chimes are playing
  'The conquering hero comes',

Come you home a hero,
  Or come not home at all,
The lads you leave will mind you
  Till Ludlow tower shall fall.

And you will list the bugle
  That blows in lands of morn,
And make the foes of England
  Be sorry you were born.

12

And you till trump of doomsday
  On lands of morn may lie,
And make the hearts of comrades
  Be heavy where you die.

Leave your home behind you,
  Your friends by field and town:
Oh, town and field will mind you
  Till Ludlow tower is down.

IV

REVEILLE

Wake: the silver dusk returning
  Up the beach of darkness brims,
And the ship of sunrise burning
  Strands upon the eastern rims.

Wake: the vaulted shadow shatters,
  Trampled to the floor it spanned,
And the tent of night in tatters
  Straws the sky-pavilioned land.

Up, lad, up, 'tis late for lying:
  Hear the drums of morning play;
Hark, the empty highways crying
  'Who'll beyond the hills away?'

Towns and countries woo together,
  Forelands beacon, belfries call;
Never lad that trod on leather
  Lived to feast his heart with all.

Up, lad: thews that lie and cumber
  Sunlit pallets never thrive;
Morns abed and daylight slumber
  Were not meant for man alive.

Clay lies still, but blood's a rover;
  Breath's a ware that will not keep.
Up, lad: when the journey's over
  There'll be time enough to sleep.

V

Oh see how thick the goldcup flowers
    Are lying in field and lane,
With dandelions to tell the hours
    That never are told again.
Oh may I squire you round the meads
    And pick you posies gay?
— 'Twill do no harm to take my arm.
    'You may, young man, you may.'

Ah, spring was sent for lass and lad,
    'Tis now the blood runs gold,
And man and maid had best be glad
    Before the world is old.
What flowers to-day may flower to-morrow,
    But never as good as new.
— Suppose I wound my arm right round —
    ' 'Tis true, young man, 'tis true.'

Some lads there are, 'tis shame to say,
    That only court to thieve,
And once they bear the bloom away
    'Tis little enough they leave.
Then keep your heart for men like me
    And safe from trustless chaps.
My love is true and all for you.
    'Perhaps, young man, perhaps.'

Oh, look in my eyes then, can you doubt?
   — Why, 'tis a mile from town.
How green the grass is all about!
   We might as well sit down.
— Ah, life, what is it but a flower?
   Why must true lovers sigh?
Be kind, have pity, my own, my pretty, —
   'Good-bye, young man, good-bye.'

V I

When the lad for longing sighs,
  Mute and dull of cheer and pale,
If at death's own door he lies,
  Maiden, you can heal his ail.

Lovers' ills are all to buy:
  The wan look, the hollow tone,
The hung head, the sunken eye,
  You can have them for your own.

Buy them, buy them: eve and morn
  Lovers' ills are all to sell.
Then you can lie down forlorn;
  But the lover will be well.

VII

When smoke stood up from Ludlow,
    And mist blew off from Teme,
And blithe afield to ploughing
    Against the morning beam
    I strode beside my team,

The blackbird in the coppice
    Looked out to see me stride,
And hearkened as I whistled
    The trampling team beside,
    And fluted and replied:

'Lie down, lie down, young yeoman;
    What use to rise and rise?
Rise man a thousand mornings
    Yet down at last he lies,
    And then the man is wise.'

I heard the tune he sang me,
    And spied his yellow bill;
I picked a stone and aimed it
    And threw it with a will:
    Then the bird was still.

Then my soul within me
  Took up the blackbird's strain,
And still beside the horses
  Along the dewy lane
  It sang the song again:

'Lie down, lie down, young yeoman;
  The sun moves always west;
The road one treads to labour
  Will lead one home to rest,
  And that will be the best.'

VIII

'Farewell to barn and stack and tree,
    Farewell to Severn shore.
Terence, look your last at me,
    For I come home no more.

'The sun burns on the half-mown hill,
    By now the blood is dried;
And Maurice amongst the hay lies still
    And my knife is in his side.

'My mother thinks us long away;
    'Tis time the field were mown.
She had two sons at rising day,
    To-night she'll be alone.

'And here's a bloody hand to shake,
    And oh, man, here's good-bye;
We'll sweat no more on scythe and rake,
    My bloody hands and I.

'I wish you strength to bring you pride,
    And a love to keep you clean,
And I wish you luck, come Lammastide,
    At racing on the green.

'Long for me the rick will wait,
    And long will wait the fold,
And long will stand the empty plate,
    And dinner will be cold.'

IX

On moonlit heath and lonesome bank
   The sheep beside me graze;
And yon the gallows used to clank
   Fast by the four cross ways.

A careless shepherd once would keep
   The flocks by moonlight there,[1]
And high amongst the glimmering sheep
   The dead man stood on air.

They hang us now in Shrewsbury jail:
   The whistles blow forlorn,
And trains all night groan on the rail
   To men that die at morn.

There sleeps in Shrewsbury jail to-night,
   Or wakes, as may betide,
A better lad, if things went right,
   Than most that sleep outside.

And naked to the hangman's noose
   The morning clocks will ring
A neck God made for other use
   Than strangling in a string.

[1] Hanging in chains was called keeping sheep by moonlight.

And sharp the link of life will snap,
   And dead on air will stand
Heels that held up as straight a chap
   As treads upon the land.

So here I'll watch the night and wait
   To see the morning shine,
When he will hear the stroke of eight
   And not the stroke of nine;

And wish my friend as sound a sleep
   As lads' I did not know,
That shepherded the moonlit sheep
   A hundred years ago.

X

MARCH

The Sun at noon to higher air,
Unharnessing the silver Pair
That late before his chariot swam,
Rides on the gold wool of the Ram.

So braver notes the storm-cock sings
To start the rusted wheel of things,
And brutes in field and brutes in pen
Leap that the world goes round again.

The boys are up the woods with day
To fetch the daffodils away,
And home at noonday from the hills
They bring no dearth of daffodils.

Afield for palms the girls repair,
And sure enough the palms are there,
And each will find by hedge or pond
Her waving silver-tufted wand.

In farm and field through all the shire
The eye beholds the heart's desire;
Ah, let not only mine be vain,
For lovers should be loved again.

XI

On your midnight pallet lying,
    Listen, and undo the door:
Lads that waste the light in sighing
    In the dark should sigh no more;
Night should ease a lover's sorrow;
Therefore, since I go to-morrow,
    Pity me before.

In the land to which I travel,
    The far dwelling, let me say —
Once, if here the couch is gravel,
    In a kinder bed I lay,
And the breast the darnel smothers
Rested once upon another's
    When it was not clay.

XII

When I watch the living meet,
    And the moving pageant file
Warm and breathing through the street
    Where I lodge a little while,

If the heats of hate and lust
    In the house of flesh are strong,
Let me mind the house of dust
    Where my sojourn shall be long.

In the nation that is not
    Nothing stands that stood before;
There revenges are forgot,
    And the hater hates no more;

Lovers lying two and two
    Ask not whom they sleep beside,
And the bridegroom all night through
    Never turns him to the bride.

XIII

When I was one-and-twenty
   I heard a wise man say,
'Give crowns and pounds and guineas
   But not your heart away;
Give pearls away and rubies
   But keep your fancy free.'
But I was one-and-twenty,
   No use to talk to me.

When I was one-and-twenty
   I heard him say again,
'The heart out of the bosom
   Was never given in vain;
'Tis paid with sighs a plenty
   And sold for endless rue.'
And I am two-and-twenty,
   And oh, 'tis true, 'tis true.

XIV

There pass the careless people
    That call their souls their own:
Here by the road I loiter,
    How idle and alone.

Ah, past the plunge of plummet,
    In seas I cannot sound,
My heart and soul and senses,
    World without end, are drowned.

His folly has not fellow
    Beneath the blue of day
That gives to man or woman
    His heart and soul away.

There flowers no balm to sain him
    From east of earth to west
That's lost for everlasting
    The heart out of his breast.

Here by the labouring highway
    With empty hands I stroll:
Sea-deep, till doomsday morning,
    Lie lost my heart and soul.

XV

Look not in my eyes, for fear
   They mirror true the sight I see,
And there you find your face too clear
   And love it and be lost like me.
One the long nights through must lie
   Spent in star-defeated sighs,
But why should you as well as I
   Perish? gaze not in my eyes.

A Grecian lad, as I hear tell,
   One that many loved in vain,
Looked into a forest well
   And never looked away again.
There, when the turf in springtime flowers,
   With downward eye and gazes sad,
Stands amid the glancing showers
   A jonquil, not a Grecian lad.

XVI

It nods and curtseys and recovers
  When the wind blows above,
The nettle on the graves of lovers
  That hanged themselves for love.

The nettle nods, the wind blows over,
  The man, he does not move,
The lover of the grave, the lover
  That hanged himself for love.

XVII

Twice a week the winter thorough
   Here stood I to keep the goal:
Football then was fighting sorrow
   For the young man's soul.

Now in Maytime to the wicket
   Out I march with bat and pad:
See the son of grief at cricket
   Trying to be glad.

Try I will; no harm in trying:
   Wonder 'tis how little mirth
Keeps the bones of man from lying
   On the bed of earth.

XVIII

Oh, when I was in love with you,
  Then I was clean and brave,
And miles around the wonder grew
  How well did I behave.

And now the fancy passes by,
  And nothing will remain,
And miles around they'll say that I
  Am quite myself again.

XIX

TO AN ATHLETE DYING YOUNG

The time you won your town the race
We chaired you through the market-place;
Man and boy stood cheering by,
And home we brought you shoulder-high.

To-day, the road all runners come,
Shoulder-high we bring you home,
And set you at your threshold down,
Townsman of a stiller town.

Smart lad, to slip betimes away
From fields where glory does not stay
And early though the laurel grows
It withers quicker than the rose.

Eyes the shady night has shut
Cannot see the record cut,
And silence sounds no worse than cheers
After earth has stopped the ears:

Now you will not swell the rout
Of lads that wore their honours out,
Runners whom renown outran
And the name died before the man.

So set, before its echoes fade,
The fleet foot on the sill of shade,
And hold to the low lintel up
The still-defended challenge-cup.

And round that early-laurelled head
Will flock to gaze the strengthless dead,
And find unwithered on its curls
The garland briefer than a girl's.

X X

Oh fair enough are sky and plain,
    But I know fairer far:
Those are as beautiful again
    That in the water are;

The pools and rivers wash so clean
    The trees and clouds and air,
The like on earth was never seen,
    And oh that I were there.

These are the thoughts I often think
    As I stand gazing down
In act upon the cressy brink
    To strip and dive and drown;

But in the golden-sanded brooks
    And azure meres I spy
A silly lad that longs and looks
    And wishes he were I.

XXI

BREDON[1] HILL

In summertime on Bredon
   The bells they sound so clear;
Round both the shires they ring them
   In steeples far and near,
   A happy noise to hear.

Here of a Sunday morning
   My love and I would lie,
And see the coloured counties,
   And hear the larks so high
   About us in the sky.

The bells would ring to call her
   In valleys miles away:
'Come all to church, good people;
   Good people, come and pray.'
   But here my love would stay.

And I would turn and answer
   Among the springing thyme,
'Oh, peal upon our wedding,
   And we will hear the chime,
   And come to church in time.'

[1] Pronounced Breedon.

But when the snows at Christmas
    On Bredon top were strown,
My love rose up so early
    And stole out unbeknown
    And went to church alone.

They tolled the one bell only,
    Groom there was none to see,
The mourners followed after,
    And so to church went she,
    And would not wait for me.

The bells they sound on Bredon,
    And still the steeples hum.
'Come all to church, good people,' —
    Oh, noisy bells, be dumb;
    I hear you, I will come.

XXII

The street sounds to the soldiers' tread,
   And out we troop to see:
A single redcoat turns his head,
   He turns and looks at me.

My man, from sky to sky's so far,
   We never crossed before;
Such leagues apart the world's ends are,
   We're like to meet no more;

What thoughts at heart have you and I
   We cannot stop to tell;
But dead or living, drunk or dry,
   Soldier, I wish you well.

XXIII

The lads in their hundreds to Ludlow come in for the fair,
    There's men from the barn and the forge and the mill and
        the fold,
The lads for the girls and the lads for the liquor are there,
    And there with the rest are the lads that will never be old.

There's chaps from the town and the field and the till and the
        cart,
    And many to count are the stalwart, and many the brave,
And many the handsome of face and the handsome of heart,
    And few that will carry their looks or their truth to the
        grave.

I wish one could know them, I wish there were tokens to tell
    The fortunate fellows that now you can never discern;
And then one could talk with them friendly and wish them
        farewell
    And watch them depart on the way that they will not re-
        turn.

But now you may stare as you like and there's nothing to scan;
    And brushing your elbow unguessed-at and not to be told
They carry back bright to the coiner the mintage of man,
    The lads that will die in their glory and never be old.

XXIV

Say, lad, have you things to do?
   Quick then, while your day's at prime.
Quick, and if 'tis work for two,
   Here am I, man: now's your time.

Send me now, and I shall go;
   Call me, I shall hear you call;
Use me ere they lay me low
   Where a man's no use at all;

Ere the wholesome flesh decay,
   And the willing nerve be numb,
And the lips lack breath to say,
   'No, my lad, I cannot come.'

XXV

This time of year a twelvemonth past,
   When Fred and I would meet,
We needs must jangle, till at last
   We fought and I was beat.

So then the summer fields about,
   Till rainy days began,
Rose Harland on her Sundays out
   Walked with the better man.

The better man she walks with still,
   Though now 'tis not with Fred:
A lad that lives and has his will
   Is worth a dozen dead.

Fred keeps the house all kinds of weather,
   And clay's the house he keeps;
When Rose and I walk out together
   Stock-still lies Fred and sleeps.

XXVI

Along the field as we came by
A year ago, my love and I,
The aspen over stile and stone
Was talking to itself alone.
'Oh who are these that kiss and pass?
A country lover and his lass;
Two lovers looking to be wed;
And time shall put them both to bed,
But she shall lie with earth above,
And he beside another love.'

And sure enough beneath the tree
There walks another love with me,
And overhead the aspen heaves
Its rainy-sounding silver leaves;
And I spell nothing in their stir,
But now perhaps they speak to her,
And plain for her to understand
They talk about a time at hand
When I shall sleep with clover clad,
And she beside another lad.

XXVII

'Is my team ploughing,
  That I was used to drive
And hear the harness jingle
  When I was man alive?'

Ay, the horses trample,
  The harness jingles now;
No change though you lie under
  The land you used to plough.

'Is football playing
  Along the river shore,
With lads to chase the leather,
  Now I stand up no more?'

Ay, the ball is flying,
  The lads play heart and soul;
The goal stands up, the keeper
  Stands up to keep the goal.

'Is my girl happy,
  That I thought hard to leave,
And has she tired of weeping
  As she lies down at eve?'

Ay, she lies down lightly,
  She lies not down to weep:
Your girl is well contented.
  Be still, my lad, and sleep.

'Is my friend hearty,
   Now I am thin and pine,
And has he found to sleep in
   A better bed than mine?'

Yes, lad, I lie easy,
   I lie as lads would choose;
I cheer a dead man's sweetheart,
   Never ask me whose.

XXVIII

THE WELSH MARCHES

High the vanes of Shrewsbury gleam
Islanded in Severn stream;
The bridges from the steepled crest
Cross the water east and west.

The flag of morn in conqueror's state
Enters at the English gate:
The vanquished eve, as night prevails,
Bleeds upon the road to Wales.

Ages since the vanquished bled
Round my mother's marriage-bed;
There the ravens feasted far
About the open house of war:

When Severn down to Buildwas ran
Coloured with the death of man,
Couched upon her brother's grave
The Saxon got me on the slave.

The sound of fight is silent long
That began the ancient wrong;
Long the voice of tears is still
That wept of old the endless ill.

In my heart it has not died,
The war that sleeps on Severn side;
They cease not fighting, east and west,
On the marches of my breast.

Here the truceless armies yet
Trample, rolled in blood and sweat;
They kill and kill and never die;
And I think that each is I.

None will part us, none undo
The knot that makes one flesh of two,
Sick with hatred, sick with pain,
Strangling — When shall we be slain?

When shall I be dead and rid
Of the wrong my father did?
How long, how long, till spade and hearse
Put to sleep my mother's curse?

XXIX

THE LENT LILY

'Tis spring; come out to ramble
    The hilly brakes around,
For under thorn and bramble
    About the hollow ground
    The primroses are found.

And there's the windflower chilly
    With all the winds at play,
And there's the Lenten lily
    That has not long to stay
    And dies on Easter day.

And since till girls go maying
    You find the primrose still,
And find the windflower playing
    With every wind at will,
    But not the daffodil,

Bring baskets now, and sally
    Upon the spring's array,
And bear from hill and valley
    The daffodil away
    That dies on Easter day.

X X X

Others, I am not the first,
Have willed more mischief than they durst:
If in the breathless night I too
Shiver now, 'tis nothing new.

More than I, if truth were told,
Have stood and sweated hot and cold,
And through their reins in ice and fire
Fear contended with desire.

Agued once like me were they,
But I like them shall win my way
Lastly to the bed of mould
Where there's neither heat nor cold.

But from my grave across my brow
Plays no wind of healing now,
And fire and ice within me fight
Beneath the suffocating night.

XXXI

On Wenlock Edge the wood's in trouble;
  His forest fleece the Wrekin heaves;
The gale, it plies the saplings double,
  And thick on Severn snow the leaves.

'Twould blow like this through holt and hanger
  When Uricon the city stood:
'Tis the old wind in the old anger,
  But then it threshed another wood.

Then, 'twas before my time, the Roman
  At yonder heaving hill would stare:
The blood that warms an English yeoman,
  The thoughts that hurt him, they were there.

There, like the wind through woods in riot,
  Through him the gale of life blew high;
The tree of man was never quiet:
  Then 'twas the Roman, now 'tis I.

The gale, it plies the saplings double,
  It blows so hard, 'twill soon be gone:
To-day the Roman and his trouble
  Are ashes under Uricon.

XXXII

From far, from eve and morning
    And yon twelve-winded sky,
The stuff of life to knit me
    Blew hither: here am I.

Now — for a breath I tarry
    Nor yet disperse apart —
Take my hand quick and tell me,
    What have you in your heart.

Speak now, and I will answer;
    How shall I help you, say;
Ere to the wind's twelve quarters
    I take my endless way.

XXXIII

If truth in hearts that perish
   Could move the powers on high,
I think the love I bear you
   Should make you not to die.

Sure, sure, if stedfast meaning,
   If single thought could save,
The world might end to-morrow,
   You should not see the grave.

This long and sure-set liking,
   This boundless will to please,
— Oh, you should live for ever
   If there were help in these.

But now, since all is idle,
   To this lost heart be kind,
Ere to a town you journey
   Where friends are ill to find.

XXXIV

THE NEW MISTRESS

'Oh, sick I am to see you, will you never let me be?
You may be good for something but you are not good for me.
Oh, go where you are wanted, for you are not wanted here.
And that was all the farewell when I parted from my dear.

'I will go where I am wanted, to a lady born and bred
Who will dress me free for nothing in a uniform of red;
She will not be sick to see me if I only keep it clean:
I will go where I am wanted for a soldier of the Queen.

'I will go where I am wanted, for the sergeant does not mind;
He may be sick to see me but he treats me very kind:
He gives me beer and breakfast and a ribbon for my cap,
And I never knew a sweetheart spend her money on a chap.

'I will go where I am wanted, where there's room for one or
       two,
And the men are none too many for the work there is to do;
Where the standing line wears thinner and the dropping dead
       lie thick;
And the enemies of England they shall see me and be sick.'

X X X V

On the idle hill of summer,
　Sleepy with the flow of streams,
Far I hear the steady drummer
　Drumming like a noise in dreams.

Far and near and low and louder
　On the roads of earth go by,
Dear to friends and food for powder,
　Soldiers marching, all to die.

East and west on fields forgotten
　Bleach the bones of comrades slain,
Lovely lads and dead and rotten;
　None that go return again.

Far the calling bugles hollo,
　High the screaming fife replies,
Gay the files of scarlet follow:
　Woman bore me, I will rise.

XXXVI

White in the moon the long road lies,
  The moon stands blank above;
White in the moon the long road lies
  That leads me from my love.

Still hangs the hedge without a gust,
  Still, still the shadows stay:
My feet upon the moonlit dust
  Pursue the ceaseless way.

The world is round, so travellers tell,
  And straight though reach the track,
Trudge on, trudge on, 'twill all be well,
  The way will guide one back.

But ere the circle homeward hies
  Far, far must it remove:
White in the moon the long road lies
  That leads me from my love.

XXXVII

As through the wild green hills of Wyre
The train ran, changing sky and shire,
And far behind, a fading crest,
Low in the forsaken west
Sank the high-reared head of Clee,
My hand lay empty on my knee.
Aching on my knee it lay:
That morning half a shire away
So many an honest fellow's fist
Had well-nigh wrung it from the wrist.
Hand, said I, since now we part
From fields and men we know by heart,
For strangers' faces, strangers' lands,—
Hand, you have held true fellows' hands.
Be clean then; rot before you do
A thing they'd not believe of you.
You and I must keep from shame
In London streets the Shropshire name;
On banks of Thames they must not say
Severn breeds worse men than they;
And friends abroad must bear in mind
Friends at home they leave behind.
Oh, I shall be stiff and cold
When I forget you, hearts of gold;
The land where I shall mind you not
Is the land where all's forgot.

And if my foot returns no more
To Teme nor Corve nor Severn shore,
Luck, my lads, be with you still
By falling stream and standing hill,
By chiming tower and whispering tree,
Men that made a man of me.
About your work in town and farm
Still you'll keep my head from harm,
Still you'll help me, hands that gave
A grasp to friend me to the grave.

XXXVIII

The winds out of the west land blow,
   My friends have breathed them there;
Warm with the blood of lads I know
   Comes east the sighing air.

It fanned their temples, filled their lungs,
   Scattered their forelocks free;
My friends made words of it with tongues
   That talk no more to me.

Their voices, dying as they fly,
   Loose on the wind are sown;
The names of men blow soundless by,
   My fellows' and my own.

Oh lads, at home I heard you plain,
   But here your speech is still,
And down the sighing wind in vain
   You hollo from the hill.

The wind and I, we both were there,
   But neither long abode;
Now through the friendless world we fare
   And sigh upon the road.

XXXIX

'Tis time, I think, by Wenlock town
    The golden broom should blow;
The hawthorn sprinkled up and down
    Should charge the land with snow.

Spring will not wait the loiterer's time
    Who keeps so long away;
So others wear the broom and climb
    The hedgerows heaped with may.

Oh tarnish late on Wenlock Edge,
    Gold that I never see;
Lie long, high snowdrifts in the hedge
    That will not shower on me.

X L

Into my heart an air that kills
   From yon far country blows:
What are those blue remembered hills,
   What spires, what farms are those?

That is the land of lost content,
   I see it shining plain,
The happy highways where I went
   And cannot come again.

XLI

In my own shire, if I was sad,
Homely comforters I had:
The earth, because my heart was sore,
Sorrowed for the son she bore;
And standing hills, long to remain,
Shared their short-lived comrade's pain.
And bound for the same bourn as I,
On every road I wandered by,
Trod beside me, close and dear,
The beautiful and death-struck year:
Whether in the woodland brown
I heard the beechnut rustle down,
And saw the purple crocus pale
Flower about the autumn dale;
Or littering far the fields of May
Lady-smocks a-bleaching lay,
And like a skylit water stood
The bluebells in the azured wood.

Yonder, lightening other loads,
The seasons range the country roads,
But here in London streets I ken
No such helpmates, only men;
And these are not in plight to bear,
If they would, another's care.

They have enough as 'tis: I see
In many an eye that measures me
The mortal sickness of a mind
Too unhappy to be kind.
Undone with misery, all they can
Is to hate their fellow man;
And till they drop they needs must still
Look at you and wish you ill.

XLII

THE MERRY GUIDE

Once in the wind of morning
I ranged the thymy wold;
The world-wide air was azure
And all the brooks ran gold.

There through the dews beside me
Behold a youth that trod,
With feathered cap on forehead,
And poised a golden rod.

With mien to match the morning
And gay delightful guise
And friendly brows and laughter
He looked me in the eyes.

Oh whence, I asked, and whither?
He smiled and would not say,
And looked at me and beckoned
And laughed and led the way.

And with kind looks and laughter
And nought to say beside
We two went on together,
I and my happy guide.

Across the glittering pastures
    And empty upland still
And solitude of shepherds
    High in the folded hill,

By hanging woods and hamlets
    That gaze through orchards down
On many a windmill turning
    And far-discovered town,

With gay regards of promise
    And sure unslackened stride
And smiles and nothing spoken
    Led on my merry guide.

By blowing realms of woodland
    With sunstruck vanes afield
And cloud-led shadows sailing
    About the windy weald,

By valley-guarded granges
    And silver waters wide,
Content at heart I followed
    With my delightful guide.

And like the cloudy shadows
    Across the country blown
We two fare on for ever,
    But not we two alone.

With the great gale we journey
   That breathes from gardens thinned,
Borne in the drift of blossoms
   Whose petals throng the wind;

Buoyed on the heaven-heard whisper
   Of dancing leaflets whirled
From all the woods that autumn
   Bereaves in all the world.

And midst the fluttering legion
   Of all that ever died
I follow, and before us
   Goes the delightful guide,

With lips that brim with laughter
   But never once respond,
And feet that fly on feathers,
   And serpent-circled wand.

XLIII

THE IMMORTAL PART

When I meet the morning beam
Or lay me down at night to dream,
I hear my bones within me say,
'Another night, another day.

'When shall this slough of sense be cast,
This dust of thoughts be laid at last,
The man of flesh and soul be slain
And the man of bone remain?

'This tongue that talks, these lungs that shout,
These thews that hustle us about,
This brain that fills the skull with schemes,
And its humming hive of dreams,—

'These to-day are proud in power
And lord it in their little hour:
The immortal bones obey control
Of dying flesh and dying soul.

' 'Tis long till eve and morn are gone:
Slow the endless night comes on,
And late to fulness grows the birth
That shall last as long as earth.

'Wanderers eastward, wanderers west,
Know you why you cannot rest?
'Tis that every mother's son
Travails with a skeleton.

'Lie down in the bed of dust;
Bear the fruit that bear you must;
Bring the eternal seed to light,
And morn is all the same as night.

'Rest you so from trouble sore,
Fear the heat o' the sun no more,
Nor the snowing winter wild,
Now you labour not with child.

'Empty vessel, garment cast,
We that wore you long shall last.
— Another night, another day.'
So my bones within me say.

Therefore they shall do my will
To-day while I am master still,
And flesh and soul, now both are strong,
Shall hale the sullen slaves along,

Before this fire of sense decay,
This smoke of thought blow clean away,
And leave with ancient night alone
The stedfast and enduring bone.

XLIV

Shot? so quick, so clean an ending?
    Oh that was right, lad, that was brave:
Yours was not an ill for mending,
    'Twas best to take it to the grave.

Oh you had forethought, you could reason,
    And saw your road and where it led,
And early wise and brave in season
    Put the pistol to your head.

Oh soon, and better so than later
    After long disgrace and scorn,
You shot dead the household traitor,
    The soul that should not have been born.

Right you guessed the rising morrow
    And scorned to tread the mire you must:
Dust's your wages, son of sorrow,
    But men may come to worse than dust.

Souls undone, undoing others, —
    Long time since the tale began.
You would not live to wrong your brothers:
    Oh lad, you died as fits a man.

Now to your grave shall friend and stranger
  With ruth and some with envy come:
Undishonoured, clear of danger,
  Clean of guilt, pass hence and home.

Turn safe to rest, no dreams, no waking;
  And here, man, here's the wreath I've made:
'Tis not a gift that's worth the taking,
  But wear it and it will not fade.

XLV

If it chance your eye offend you,
  Pluck it out, lad, and be sound:
'Twill hurt, but here are salves to friend you,
  And many a balsam grows on ground.

And if your hand or foot offend you,
  Cut it off, lad, and be whole;
But play the man, stand up and end you,
  When your sickness is your soul.

XLVI

Bring, in this timeless grave to throw,
No cypress, sombre on the snow;
Snap not from the bitter yew
His leaves that live December through;
Break no rosemary, bright with rime
And sparkling to the cruel clime;
Nor plod the winter land to look
For willows in the icy brook
To cast them leafless round him: bring
No spray that ever buds in spring.

But if the Christmas field has kept
Awns the last gleaner overstept,
Or shrivelled flax, whose flower is blue
A single season, never two;
Or if one haulm whose year is o'er
Shivers on the upland frore,
— Oh, bring from hill and stream and plain
Whatever will not flower again,
To give him comfort: he and those
Shall bide eternal bedfellows
Where low upon the couch he lies
Whence he never shall arise.

XLVII

THE CARPENTER'S SON

'Here the hangman stops his cart:
Now the best of friends must part.
Fare you well, for ill fare I:
Live, lads, and I will die.

'Oh, at home had I but stayed
'Prenticed to my father's trade,
Had I stuck to plane and adze,
I had not been lost, my lads.

'Then I might have built perhaps
Gallows-trees for other chaps,
Never dangled on my own,
Had I but left ill alone.

'Now, you see, they hang me high,
And the people passing by
Stop to shake their fists and curse;
So 'tis come from ill to worse.

'Here hang I, and right and left
Two poor fellows hang for theft:
All the same's the luck we prove,
Though the midmost hangs for love.

'Comrades all, that stand and gaze,
Walk henceforth in other ways;
See my neck and save your own:
Comrades all, leave ill alone.

'Make some day a decent end,
Shrewder fellows than your friend.
Fare you well, for ill fare I:
Live, lads, and I will die.'

XLVIII

Be still, my soul, be still; the arms you bear are brittle,
   Earth and high heaven are fixt of old and founded
     strong.
Think rather, — call to thought, if now you grieve a little,
   The days when we had rest, O soul, for they were long.

Men loved unkindness then, but lightless in the quarry
   I slept and saw not; tears fell down, I did not mourn;
Sweat ran and blood sprang out and I was never sorry:
   Then it was well with me, in days ere I was born.

Now, and I muse for why and never find the reason,
   I pace the earth, and drink the air, and feel the sun.
Be still, be still, my soul; it is but for a season:
   Let us endure an hour and see injustice done.

Ay, look: high heaven and earth ail from the prime
     foundation;
   All thoughts to rive the heart are here, and all are vain:
Horror and scorn and hate and fear and indignation —
   Oh why did I awake? when shall I sleep again?

XLIX

Think no more, lad; laugh, be jolly:
  Why should men make haste to die?
Empty heads and tongues a-talking
Make the rough road easy walking,
And the feather pate of folly
  Bears the falling sky.

Oh, 'tis jesting, dancing, drinking
  Spins the heavy world around.
If young hearts were not so clever,
Oh, they would be young for ever:
Think no more; 'tis only thinking
  Lays lads underground.

L

Clunton and Clunbury,
  Clungunford and Clun,
Are the quietest places
  Under the sun.

In valleys of springs of rivers,
  By Ony and Teme and Clun,
The country for easy livers,
  The quietest under the sun,

We still had sorrows to lighten,
  One could not be always glad,
And lads knew trouble at Knighton
  When I was a Knighton lad.

By bridges that Thames runs under,
  In London, the town built ill,
'Tis sure small matter for wonder
  If sorrow is with one still.

And if as a lad grows older
  The troubles he bears are more,
He carries his griefs on a shoulder
  That handselled them long before.

Where shall one halt to deliver
   This luggage I'd lief set down?
Not Thames, not Teme is the river,
   Nor London nor Knighton the town:

'Tis a long way further than Knighton,
   A quieter place than Clun,
Where doomsday may thunder and lighten
   And little 'twill matter to one.

L I

Loitering with a vacant eye
Along the Grecian gallery,
And brooding on my heavy ill,
I met a statue standing still.
Still in marble stone stood he,
And stedfastly he looked at me.
'Well met,' I thought the look would say,
'We both were fashioned far away;
We neither knew, when we were young,
These Londoners we live among.'

Still he stood and eyed me hard,
An earnest and a grave regard:
'What, lad, drooping with your lot?
I too would be where I am not.
I too survey that endless line
Of men whose thoughts are not as mine.
Years, ere you stood up from rest,
On my neck the collar prest;
Years, when you lay down your ill,
I shall stand and bear it still.
Courage, lad, 'tis not for long:
Stand, quit you like stone, be strong.'
So I thought his look would say;
And light on me my trouble lay,
And I stept out in flesh and bone
Manful like the man of stone.

LII

Far in a western brookland
  That bred me long ago
The poplars stand and tremble
  By pools I used to know.

There, in the windless night-time,
  The wanderer, marvelling why,
Halts on the bridge to hearken
  How soft the poplars sigh.

He hears: no more remembered
  In fields where I was known,
Here I lie down in London
  And turn to rest alone.

There, by the starlit fences,
  The wanderer halts and hears
My soul that lingers sighing
  About the glimmering weirs.

LIII

THE TRUE LOVER

The lad came to the door at night,
  When lovers crown their vows,
And whistled soft and out of sight
  In shadow of the boughs.

'I shall not vex you with my face
  Henceforth, my love, for aye;
So take me in your arms a space
  Before the east is grey.

'When I from hence away am past
  I shall not find a bride,
And you shall be the first and last
  I ever lay beside.'

She heard and went and knew not why;
  Her heart to his she laid;
Light was the air beneath the sky
  But dark under the shade.

'Oh do you breathe, lad, that your breast
  Seems not to rise and fall,
And here upon my bosom prest
  There beats no heart at all?'

78

'Oh loud, my girl, it once would knock,
   You should have felt it then;
But since for you I stopped the clock
   It never goes again.'

'Oh lad, what is it, lad, that drips
   Wet from your neck on mine?
What is it falling on my lips,
   My lad, that tastes of brine?'

'Oh like enough 'tis blood, my dear,
   For when the knife has slit
The throat across from ear to ear
   'Twill bleed because of it.'

Under the stars the air was light
   But dark below the boughs,
The still air of the speechless night,
   When lovers crown their vows.

LIV

With rue my heart is laden
  For golden friends I had,
For many a rose-lipt maiden
  And many a lightfoot lad.

By brooks too broad for leaping
  The lightfoot boys are laid;
The rose-lipt girls are sleeping
  In fields where roses fade.

L V

Westward on the high-hilled plains
  Where for me the world began,
Still, I think, in newer veins
  Frets the changeless blood of man.

Now that other lads than I
  Strip to bathe on Severn shore,
They, no help, for all they try,
  Tread the mill I trod before.

There, when hueless is the west
  And the darkness hushes wide,
Where the lad lies down to rest
  Stands the troubled dream beside.

There, on thoughts that once were mine,
  Day looks down the eastern steep,
And the youth at morning shine
  Makes the vow he will not keep.

LVI

THE DAY OF BATTLE

'Far I hear the bugle blow
To call me where I would not go,
And the guns begin the song,
"Soldier, fly or stay for long."

'Comrade, if to turn and fly
Made a soldier never die,
Fly I would, for who would not?
'Tis sure no pleasure to be shot.

'But since the man that runs away
Lives to die another day,
And cowards' funerals, when they come,
Are not wept so well at home,

'Therefore, though the best is bad,
Stand and do the best, my lad;
Stand and fight and see your slain,
And take the bullet in your brain.'

LVII

You smile upon your friend to-day,
  To-day his ills are over;
You hearken to the lover's say,
  And happy is the lover.

'Tis late to hearken, late to smile,
  But better late than never:
I shall have lived a little while
  Before I die for ever.

LVIII

When I came last to Ludlow
  Amidst the moonlight pale,
Two friends kept step beside me,
  Two honest lads and hale.

Now Dick lies long in the churchyard,
  And Ned lies long in jail,
And I come home to Ludlow
  Amidst the moonlight pale.

LIX

THE ISLE OF PORTLAND

The star-filled seas are smooth to-night
   From France to England strown;
Black towers above the Portland light
   The felon-quarried stone.

On yonder island, not to rise,
   Never to stir forth free,
Far from his folk a dead lad lies
   That once was friends with me.

Lie you easy, dream you light,
   And sleep you fast for aye;
And luckier may you find the night
   Than ever you found the day.

L X

Now hollow fires burn out to black,
  And lights are guttering low:
Square your shoulders, lift your pack,
  And leave your friends and go.

Oh never fear, man, nought's to dread,
  Look not left nor right:
In all the endless road you tread
  There's nothing but the night.

LXI

HUGHLEY STEEPLE

The vane on Hughley steeple
  Veers bright, a far-known sign,
And there lie Hughley people,
  And there lie friends of mine.
Tall in their midst the tower
  Divides the shade and sun,
And the clock strikes the hour
  And tells the time to none.

To south the headstones cluster,
  The sunny mounds lie thick;
The dead are more in muster
  At Hughley than the quick.
North, for a soon-told number,
  Chill graves the sexton delves,
And steeple-shadowed slumber
  The slayers of themselves.

To north, to south, lie parted,
  With Hughley tower above,
The kind, the single-hearted,
  The lads I used to love.
And, south or north, 'tis only
  A choice of friends one knows,
And I shall ne'er be lonely
  Asleep with these or those.

LXII

'Terence, this is stupid stuff:
You eat your victuals fast enough;
There can't be much amiss, 'tis clear,
To see the rate you drink your beer.
But oh, good Lord, the verse you make,
It gives a chap the belly-ache.
The cow, the old cow, she is dead;
It sleeps well, the horned head:
We poor lads, 'tis our turn now
To hear such tunes as killed the cow.
Pretty friendship 'tis to rhyme
Your friends to death before their time
Moping melancholy mad:
Come, pipe a tune to dance to, lad.'

Why, if 'tis dancing you would be,
There's brisker pipes than poetry.
Say, for what were hop-yards meant,
Or why was Burton built on Trent?
Oh many a peer of England brews
Livelier liquor than the Muse,
And malt does more than Milton can
To justify God's ways to man.
Ale, man, ale's the stuff to drink
For fellows whom it hurts to think:

Look into the pewter pot
To see the world as the world's not.
And faith, 'tis pleasant till 'tis past:
The mischief is that 'twill not last.
Oh I have been to Ludlow fair
And left my necktie God knows where,
And carried half-way home, or near,
Pints and quarts of Ludlow beer:
Then the world seemed none so bad,
And I myself a sterling lad;
And down in lovely muck I've lain,
Happy till I woke again.
Then I saw the morning sky:
Heigho, the tale was all a lie;
The world, it was the old world yet,
I was I, my things were wet,
And nothing now remained to do
But begin the game anew.

    Therefore, since the world has still
Much good, but much less good than ill,
And while the sun and moon endure
Luck's a chance, but trouble's sure,
I'd face it as a wise man would,
And train for ill and not for good.
'Tis true, the stuff I bring for sale
Is not so brisk a brew as ale:

Out of a stem that scored the hand
I wrung it in a weary land.
But take it: if the smack is sour,
The better for the embittered hour;
It should do good to heart and head
When your soul is in my soul's stead;
And I will friend you, if I may,
In the dark and cloudy day.

There was a king reigned in the East:
There, when kings will sit to feast,
They get their fill before they think
With poisoned meat and poisoned drink.
He gathered all that springs to birth
From the many-venomed earth;
First a little, thence to more,
He sampled all her killing store;
And easy, smiling, seasoned sound,
Sate the king when healths went round.
They put arsenic in his meat
And stared aghast to watch him eat;
They poured strychnine in his cup
And shook to see him drink it up:
They shook, they stared as white's their shirt:
Them it was their poison hurt.
— I tell the tale that I heard told.
Mithridates, he died old.

LXIII

I hoed and trenched and weeded,
    And took the flowers to fair:
I brought them home unheeded;
    The hue was not the wear.

So up and down I sow them
    For lads like me to find,
When I shall lie below them,
    A dead man out of mind.

Some seed the birds devour,
    And some the season mars,
But here and there will flower
    The solitary stars,

And fields will yearly bear them
    As light-leaved spring comes on,
And luckless lads will wear them
    When I am dead and gone.

LAST POEMS

We'll to the woods no more,
The laurels all are cut,
The bowers are bare of bay
That once the Muses wore;
The year draws in the day
And soon will evening shut:
The laurels all are cut,
We'll to the woods no more.
Oh we'll no more, no more
To the leafy woods away,
To the high wild woods of laurel
And the bowers of bay no more.

I

THE WEST

Beyond the moor and mountain crest
— Comrade, look not on the west —
The sun is down and drinks away
From air and land the lees of day.

The long cloud and the single pine
Sentinel the ending line,
And out beyond it, clear and wan,
Reach the gulfs of evening on.

The son of woman turns his brow
West from forty counties now,
And, as the edge of heaven he eyes,
Thinks eternal thoughts, and sighs.

Oh wide's the world, to rest or roam,
With change abroad and cheer at home,
Fights and furloughs, talk and tale,
Company and beef and ale.

But if I front the evening sky
Silent on the west look I,
And my comrade, stride for stride,
Paces silent at my side.

97

Comrade, look not on the west:
'Twill have the heart out of your breast;
'Twill take your thoughts and sink them **far**,
Leagues beyond the sunset bar.

Oh lad, I fear that yon's the sea
Where they fished for you and me,
And there, from whence we both were ta'en,
You and I shall drown again.

Send not on your soul before
To dive from that beguiling shore,
And let not yet the swimmer leave
His clothes upon the sands of eve.

Too fast to yonder strand forlorn
We journey, to the sunken bourn,
To flush the fading tinges eyed
By other lads at eventide.

Wide is the world, to rest or roam,
And early 'tis for turning home:
Plant your heel on earth and stand,
And let's forget our native land.

When you and I are spilt on air
Long we shall be strangers there;
Friends of flesh and bone are best:
Comrade, look not on the west.

II

As I gird on for fighting
　My sword upon my thigh,
I think on old ill fortunes
　Of better men than I.

Think I, the round world over,
　What golden lads are low
With hurts not mine to mourn for
　And shames I shall not know.

What evil luck soever
　For me remains in store,
'Tis sure much finer fellows
　Have fared much worse before.

So here are things to think on
　That ought to make me brave,
As I strap on for fighting
　My sword that will not save.

III

Her strong enchantments failing,
　Her towers of fear in wreck,
Her limbecks dried of poisons
　And the knife at her neck,

The Queen of air and darkness
　Begins to shrill and cry,
'O young man, O my slayer,
　To-morrow you shall die.'

O Queen of air and darkness,
　I think 'tis truth you say,
And I shall die to-morrow;
　But you will die to-day.

IV

ILLIC JACET

Oh hard is the bed they have made him,
  And common the blanket and cheap;
But there he will lie as they laid him:
  Where else could you trust him to sleep?

To sleep when the bugle is crying
  And cravens have heard and are brave,
When mothers and sweethearts are sighing
  And lads are in love with the grave.

Oh dark is the chamber and lonely,
  And lights and companions depart;
But lief will he lose them and only
  Behold the desire of his heart.

And low is the roof, but it covers
  A sleeper content to repose;
And far from his friends and his lovers
  He lies with the sweetheart he chose.

V

GRENADIER

The Queen she sent to look for me,
　　The sergeant he did say,
'Young man, a soldier will you be
　　For thirteen pence a day?'

For thirteen pence a day did I
　　Take off the things I wore,
And I have marched to where I lie,
　　And I shall march no more.

My mouth is dry, my shirt is wet,
　　My blood runs all away,
So now I shall not die in debt
　　For thirteen pence a day.

To-morrow after new young men
　　The sergeant he must see,
For things will all be over then
　　Between the Queen and me.

And I shall have to bate my price,
　　For in the grave, they say,
Is neither knowledge nor device
　　Nor thirteen pence a day.

VI

LANCER

I 'listed at home for a lancer,
  Oh who would not sleep with the brave?
I 'listed at home for a lancer
  To ride on a horse to my grave.

And over the seas we were bidden
  A country to take and to keep;
And far with the brave I have ridden,
  And now with the brave I shall sleep.

For round me the men will be lying
  That learned me the way to behave,
And showed me my business of dying:
  Oh who would not sleep with the brave?

They ask and there is not an answer;
Says I, I will 'list for a lancer,
  Oh who would not sleep with the brave?

And I with the brave shall be sleeping
  At ease on my mattress of loam,
When back from their taking and keeping
  The squadron is riding at home.

The wind with the plumes will be playing,
    The girls will stand watching them wave,
And eyeing my comrades and saying
    Oh who would not sleep with the brave?

They ask and there is not an answer;
Says you, I will 'list for a lancer,
    Oh who would not sleep with the brave?

VII

In valleys green and still
    Where lovers wander maying
They hear from over hill
    A music playing.

Behind the drum and fife,
    Past hawthornwood and hollow,
Through earth and out of life
    The soldiers follow.

The soldier's is the trade:
    In any wind or weather
He steals the heart of maid
    And man together.

The lover and his lass
    Beneath the hawthorn lying
Have heard the soldiers pass,
    And both are sighing.

And down the distance they
    With dying note and swelling
Walk the resounding way
    To the still dwelling.

VIII

Soldier from the wars returning,
   Spoiler of the taken town,
Here is ease that asks not earning;
   Turn you in and sit you down.

Peace is come and wars are over,
   Welcome you and welcome all,
While the charger crops the clover
   And his bridle hangs in stall.

Now no more of winters biting,
   Filth in trench from fall to spring,
Summers full of sweat and fighting
   For the Kesar or the King.

Rest you, charger, rust you, bridle;
   Kings and kesars, keep your pay;
Soldier, sit you down and idle
   At the inn of night for aye.

I X

The chestnut casts his flambeaux, and the flowers
    Stream from the hawthorn on the wind away,
The doors clap to, the pane is blind with showers.
    Pass me the can, lad; there's an end of May.

There's one spoilt spring to scant our mortal lot,
    One season ruined of our little store.
May will be fine next year as like as not:
    Oh ay, but then we shall be twenty-four.

We for a certainty are not the first
    Have sat in taverns while the tempest hurled
Their hopeful plans to emptiness, and cursed
    Whatever brute and blackguard made the world.

It is in truth iniquity on high
    To cheat our sentenced souls of aught they crave,
And mar the merriment as you and I
    Fare on our long fool's-errand to the grave.

Iniquity it is; but pass the can.
    My lad, no pair of kings our mothers bore;
Our only portion is the estate of man:
    We want the moon, but we shall get no more.

If here to-day the cloud of thunder lours
    To-morrow it will hie on far behests;
The flesh will grieve on other bones than ours
    Soon, and the soul will mourn in other breasts.

The troubles of our proud and angry dust
    Are from eternity, and shall not fail.
Bear them we can, and if we can we must.
    Shoulder the sky, my lad, and drink your ale.

X

Could man be drunk for ever
   With liquor, love, or fights,
Lief should I rouse at morning
   And lief lie down of nights.

But men at whiles are sober
   And think by fits and starts,
And if they think, they fasten
   Their hands upon their hearts.

XI

Yonder see the morning blink:
　The sun is up, and up must I,
To wash and dress and eat and drink
And look at things and talk and think
　And work, and God knows why.

Oh often have I washed and dressed
　And what's to show for all my pain?
Let me lie abed and rest:
Ten thousand times I've done my best
　And all's to do again.

XII

The laws of God, the laws of man,
He may keep that will and can;
Not I: let God and man decree
Laws for themselves and not for me;
And if my ways are not as theirs
Let them mind their own affairs.
Their deeds I judge and much condemn,
Yet when did I make laws for them?
Please yourselves, say I, and they
Need only look the other way.
But no, they will not; they must still
Wrest their neighbour to their will,
And make me dance as they desire
With jail and gallows and hell-fire.
And how am I to face the odds
Of man's bedevilment and God's?
I, a stranger and afraid
In a world I never made.
They will be master, right or wrong;
Though both are foolish, both are strong.
And since, my soul, we cannot fly
To Saturn nor to Mercury,
Keep we must, if keep we can,
These foreign laws of God and man.

XIII

THE DESERTER

'What sound awakened me, I wonder,
    For now 'tis dumb.'
'Wheels on the road most like, or thunder:
    Lie down; 'twas not the drum.'

Toil at sea and two in haven
    And trouble far:
Fly, crow, away, and follow, raven,
    And all that croaks for war.

'Hark, I heard the bugle crying,
    And where am I?
My friends are up and dressed and dying,
    And I will dress and die.'

'Oh love is rare and trouble plenty
    And carrion cheap,
And daylight dear at four-and-twenty:
    Lie down again and sleep.'

'Reach me my belt and leave your prattle:
    Your hour is gone;
But my day is the day of battle,
    And that comes dawning on.

'They mow the field of man in season:
    Farewell, my fair,
And, call it truth or call it treason,
    Farewell the vows that were.'

'Ay, false heart, forsake me lightly:
    'Tis like the brave.
They find no bed to joy in rightly
    Before they find the grave.

'Their love is for their own undoing,
    And east and west
They scour about the world a-wooing
    The bullet to their breast.

'Sail away the ocean over,
    Oh sail away,
And lie there with your leaden lover
    For ever and a day.'

XIV

THE CULPRIT

The night my father got me
   His mind was not on me;
He did not plague his fancy
   To muse if I should be
   The son you see.

The day my mother bore me
   She was a fool and glad,
For all the pain I cost her,
   That she had borne the lad
   That borne she had.

My mother and my father
   Out of the light they lie;
The warrant would not find them,
   And here 'tis only I
   Shall hang so high.

Oh let not man remember
   The soul that God forgot,
But fetch the county kerchief
   And noose me in the knot,
   And I will rot.

For so the game is ended
   That should not have begun.
My father and my mother
   They had a likely son,
   And I have none.

XV

EIGHT O'CLOCK

He stood, and heard the steeple
  Sprinkle the quarters on the morning town.
One, two, three, four, to market-place and people
  It tossed them down.

Strapped, noosed, nighing his hour,
  He stood and counted them and cursed his luck;
And then the clock collected in the tower
  Its strength, and struck.

XVI

SPRING MORNING

Star and coronal and bell
    April underfoot renews,
And the hope of man as well
    Flowers among the morning dews.

Now the old come out to look,
    Winter past and winter's pains,
How the sky in pool and brook
    Glitters on the grassy plains.

Easily the gentle air
    Wafts the turning season on;
Things to comfort them are there,
    Though 'tis true the best are gone.

Now the scorned unlucky lad
    Rousing from his pillow gnawn
Mans his heart and deep and glad
    Drinks the valiant air of dawn.

Half the night he longed to die,
    Now are sown on hill and plain
Pleasures worth his while to try
    Ere he longs to die again.

Blue the sky from east to west
   Arches, and the world is wide,
Though the girl he loves the best
   Rouses from another's side.

XVII

ASTRONOMY

The Wain upon the northern steep
   Descends and lifts away.
Oh I will sit me down and weep
   For bones in Africa.

For pay and medals, name and rank,
   Things that he has not found,
He hove the Cross to heaven and sank
   The pole-star underground.

And now he does not even see
   Signs of the nadir roll
At night over the ground where he
   Is buried with the pole.

XVIII

The rain, it streams on stone and hillock,
  The boot clings to the clay.
Since all is done that's due and right
Let's home; and now, my lad, good-night,
  For I must turn away.

Good-night, my lad, for nought's eternal;
  No league of ours, for sure.
To-morrow I shall miss you less,
And ache of heart and heaviness
  Are things that time should cure.

Over the hill the highway marches
  And what's beyond is wide:
Oh soon enough will pine to nought
Remembrance and the faithful thought
  That sits the grave beside.

The skies, they are not always raining
  Nor grey the twelvemonth through;
And I shall meet good days and mirth,
And range the lovely lands of earth
  With friends no worse than you.

But oh, my man, the house is fallen
  That none can build again;
My man, how full of joy and woe
Your mother bore you years ago
  To-night to lie in the rain.

XIX

In midnights of November,
    When Dead Man's Fair is nigh,
And danger in the valley,
    And anger in the sky,

Around the huddling homesteads
    The leafless timber roars,
And the dead call the dying
    And finger at the doors.

Oh, yonder faltering fingers
    Are hands I used to hold;
Their false companion drowses
    And leaves them in the cold.

Oh, to the bed of ocean,
    To Africk and to Ind,
I will arise and follow
    Along the rainy wind.

The night goes out and under
    With all its train forlorn;
Hues in the east assemble
    And cocks crow up the morn.

The living are the living
    And dead the dead will stay,
And I will sort with comrades
    That face the beam of day.

X X

The night is freezing fast,
  To-morrow comes December;
    And winterfalls of old
Are with me from the past;
  And chiefly I remember
    How Dick would hate the cold.

Fall, winter, fall; for he,
  Prompt hand and headpiece clever,
    Has woven a winter robe,
And made of earth and sea
  His overcoat for ever,
    And wears the turning globe.

XXI

The fairies break their dances
    And leave the printed lawn,
And up from India glances
    The silver sail of dawn.

The candles burn their sockets,
    The blinds let through the day,
The young man feels his pockets
    And wonders what's to pay.

XXII

The sloe was lost in flower,
   The April elm was dim;
That was the lover's hour,
   The hour for lies and him.

If thorns are all the bower,
   If north winds freeze the fir,
Why, 'tis another's hour,
   The hour for truth and her.

XXIII

In the morning, in the morning,
    In the happy field of hay,
Oh they looked at one another
    By the light of day.

In the blue and silver morning
    On the haycock as they lay,
Oh they looked at one another
    And they looked away.

XXIV

EPITHALAMIUM

He is here, Urania's son,
Hymen come from Helicon;
God that glads the lover's heart,
He is here to join and part.
So the groomsman quits your side
And the bridegroom seeks the bride:
Friend and comrade yield you o'er
To her that hardly loves you more.

Now the sun his skyward beam
Has tilted from the Ocean stream.
Light the Indies, laggard sun:
Happy bridegroom, day is done,
And the star from Œta's steep
Calls to bed but not to sleep.

Happy bridegroom, Hesper brings
All desired and timely things.
All whom morning sends to roam,
Hesper loves to lead them home.
Home return who him behold,
Child to mother, sheep to fold,
Bird to nest from wandering wide:
Happy bridegroom, seek your bride.

Pour it out, the golden cup
Given and guarded, brimming up,
Safe through jostling markets borne
And the thicket of the thorn;
Folly spurned and danger past,
Pour it to the god at last.

Now, to smother noise and light,
Is stolen abroad the wildering night,
And the blotting shades confuse
Path and meadow full of dews;
And the high heavens, that all control,
Turn in silence round the pole.
Catch the starry beams they shed
Prospering the marriage bed,
And breed the land that reared your prime
Sons to stay the rot of time.
All is quiet, no alarms;
Nothing fear of nightly harms.
Safe you sleep on guarded ground,
And in silent circle round
The thoughts of friends keep watch and ward,
Harnessed angels, hand on sword.

XXV

THE ORACLES

'Tis mute, the word they went to hear on high Dodona
  mountain
  When winds were in the oakenshaws and all the caul-
  drons tolled,
And mute's the midland navel-stone beside the singing
  fountain,
  And echoes list to silence now where gods told lies of
  old.

I took my question to the shrine that has not ceased from
  speaking,
  The heart within, that tells the truth and tells it twice
  as plain;
And from the cave of oracles I heard the priestess shriek-
  ing
  That she and I should surely die and never live again.

Oh priestess, what you cry is clear, and sound good sense
  I think it;
  But let the screaming echoes rest, and froth your
  mouth no more.
'Tis true there's better boose than brine, but he that
  drowns must drink it;
  And oh, my lass, the news is news that men have heard
  before.

*The King with half the East at heel is marched from lands
   of morning;
   Their fighters drink the rivers up, their shafts benight
   the air.
And he that stands will die for nought, and home there's
   no returning.*
   The Spartans on the sea-wet rock sat down and combed
   their hair.

XXVI

The half-moon westers low, my love,
   And the wind brings up the rain;
And wide apart lie we, my love,
   And seas between the twain.

I know not if it rains, my love,
   In the land where you do lie;
And oh, so sound you sleep, my love,
   You know no more than I.

XXVII

The sigh that heaves the grasses
   Whence thou wilt never rise
Is of the air that passes
   And knows not if it sighs.

The diamond tears adorning
   Thy low mound on the lea,
Those are the tears of morning,
   That weeps, but not for thee.

XXVIII

Now dreary dawns the eastern light,
  And fall of eve is drear,
And cold the poor man lies at night,
  And so goes out the year.

Little is the luck I've had,
  And oh, 'tis comfort small
To think that many another lad
  Has had no luck at all.

XXIX

Wake not for the world-heard thunder
   Nor the chime that earthquakes toll.
Star may plot in heaven with planet,
Lightning rive the rock of granite,
Tempest tread the oakwood under:
   Fear not you for flesh nor soul.
Marching, fighting, victory past,
Stretch your limbs in peace at last.

Stir not for the soldiers drilling
   Nor the fever nothing cures:
Throb of drum and timbal's rattle
Call but man alive to battle,
And the fife with death-notes filling
   Screams for blood but not for yours.
Times enough you bled your best;
Sleep on now, and take your rest.

Sleep, my lad; the French are landed,
   London's burning, Windsor's down;
Clasp your cloak of earth about you,
We must man the ditch without you,
March unled and fight short-handed,
   Charge to fall and swim to drown.
Duty, friendship, bravery o'er,
Sleep away, lad; wake no more.

XXX

SINNER'S RUE

I walked alone and thinking,
  And faint the nightwind blew
And stirred on mounds at crossways
  The flower of sinner's rue.

Where the roads part they bury
  Him that his own hand slays,
And so the weed of sorrow
  Springs at the four cross ways.

By night I plucked it hueless,
  When morning broke 'twas blue:
Blue at my breast I fastened
  The flower of sinner's rue.

It seemed a herb of healing,
  A balsam and a sign,
Flower of a heart whose trouble
  Must have been worse than mine.

Dead clay that did me kindness,
  I can do none to you,
But only wear for breastknot
  The flower of sinner's rue.

XXXI

HELL GATE

Onward led the road again
Through the sad uncoloured plain
Under twilight brooding dim,
And along the utmost rim
Wall and rampart risen to sight
Cast a shadow not of night,
And beyond them seemed to glow
Bonfires lighted long ago.
And my dark conductor broke
Silence at my side and spoke,
Saying, 'You conjecture well:
Yonder is the gate of hell.'

Ill as yet the eye could see
The eternal masonry,
But beneath it on the dark
To and fro there stirred a spark.
And again the sombre guide
Knew my question, and replied:
'At hell gate the damned in turn
Pace for sentinel and burn.'

Dully at the leaden sky
Staring, and with idle eye
Measuring the listless plain,
I began to think again.

Many things I thought of then,
Battle, and the loves of men,
Cities entered, oceans crossed,
Knowledge gained and virtue lost,
Cureless folly done and said,
And the lovely way that led
To the slimepit and the mire
And the everlasting fire.
And against a smoulder dun
And a dawn without a sun
Did the nearing bastion loom,
And across the gate of gloom
Still one saw the sentry go,
Trim and burning, to and fro,
One for women to admire
In his finery of fire.
Something, as I watched him pace,
Minded me of time and place,
Soldiers of another corps
And a sentry known before.

Ever darker hell on high
Reared its strength upon the sky,
And our footfall on the track
Fetched the daunting echo back.
But the soldier pacing still
The insuperable sill,
Nursing his tormented pride,

Turned his head to neither side,
Sunk into himself apart
And the hell-fire of his heart.
But against our entering in
From the drawbridge Death and Sin
Rose to render key and sword
To their father and their lord.
And the portress foul to see
Lifted up her eyes on me
Smiling, and I made reply:
'Met again, my lass,' said I.
Then the sentry turned his head,
Looked, and knew me, and was Ned.

Once he looked, and halted straight,
Set his back against the gate,
Caught his musket to his chin,
While the hive of hell within
Sent abroad a seething hum
As of towns whose king is come
Leading conquest home from far
And the captives of his war,
And the car of triumph waits,
And they open wide the gates.
But across the entry barred
Straddled the revolted guard,
Weaponed and accoutred well
From the arsenals of hell;

And beside him, sick and white,
Sin to left and Death to right
Turned a countenance of fear
On the flaming mutineer.
Over us the darkness bowed,
And the anger in the cloud
Clenched the lightning for the stroke;
But the traitor musket spoke.

And the hollowness of hell
Sounded as its master fell,
And the mourning echo rolled
Ruin through his kingdom old.
Tyranny and terror flown
Left a pair of friends alone,
And beneath the nether sky
All that stirred was he and I.

Silent, nothing found to say,
We began the backward way;
And the ebbing lustre died
From the soldier at my side,
As in all his spruce attire
Failed the everlasting fire.
Midmost of the homeward track
Once we listened and looked back;
But the city, dusk and mute,
Slept, and there was no pursuit.

XXXII

When I would muse in boyhood
   The wild green woods among,
And nurse resolves and fancies
   Because the world was young,
It was not foes to conquer,
   Nor sweethearts to be kind,
But it was friends to die for
   That I would seek and find.

I sought them far and found them,
   The sure, the straight, the brave,
The hearts I lost my own to,
   The souls I could not save.
They braced their belts about them,
   They crossed in ships the sea,
They sought and found six feet of ground,
   And there they died for me.

XXXIII

When the eye of day is shut,
   And the stars deny their beams,
And about the forest hut
   Blows the roaring wood of dreams,

From deep clay, from desert rock,
   From the sunk sands of the main,
Come not at my door to knock,
   Hearts that loved me not again.

Sleep, be still, turn to your rest
   In the lands where you are laid;
In far lodgings east and west
   Lie down on the beds you made.

In gross marl, in blowing dust,
   In the drowned ooze of the sea,
Where you would not, lie you must,
   Lie you must, and not with me.

XXXIV

THE FIRST OF MAY

The orchards half the way
  From home to Ludlow fair
Flowered on the first of May
  In Mays when I was there;
And seen from stile or turning
  The plume of smoke would show
Where fires were burning
  That went out long ago

The plum broke forth in green,
  The pear stood high and snowed,
My friends and I between
  Would take the Ludlow road;
Dressed to the nines and drinking
  And light in heart and limb,
And each chap thinking
  The fair was held for him.

Between the trees in flower
  New friends at fairtime tread
The way where Ludlow tower
  Stands planted on the dead.
Our thoughts, a long while after,
  They think, our words they say;
Theirs now's the laughter,
  The fair, the first of May.

Ay, yonder lads are yet
   The fools that we were then;
For oh, the sons we get
   Are still the sons of men.
The sumless tale of sorrow
   Is all unrolled in vain:
May comes to-morrow
   And Ludlow fair again.

XXXV

When first my way to fair I took
   Few pence in purse had I,
And long I used to stand and look
   At things I could not buy.

Now times are altered: if I care
   To buy a thing, I can;
The pence are here and here's the fair,
   But where's the lost young man?

— To think that two and two are four
   And neither five nor three
The heart of man has long been sore
   And long 'tis like to be.

XXXVI

REVOLUTION

West and away the wheels of darkness roll,
    Day's beamy banner up the east is borne,
Spectres and fears, the nightmare and her foal,
    Drown in the golden deluge of the morn.

But over sea and continent from sight
    Safe to the Indies has the earth conveyed
The vast and moon-eclipsing cone of night,
    Her towering foolscap of eternal shade.

See, in mid heaven the sun is mounted; hark,
    The belfries tingle to the noonday chime.
'Tis silent, and the subterranean dark
    Has crossed the nadir, and begins to climb.

XXXVII

EPITAPH ON AN ARMY OF MERCENARIES

These, in the day when heaven was falling,
    The hour when earth's foundations fled,
Followed their mercenary calling
    And took their wages and are dead.

Their shoulders held the sky suspended;
    They stood, and earth's foundations stay;
What God abandoned, these defended,
    And saved the sum of things for pay.

XXXVIII

Oh stay at home, my lad, and plough
   The land and not the sea,
And leave the soldiers at their drill,
And all about the idle hill
   Shepherd your sheep with me.

Oh stay with company and mirth
   And daylight and the air;
Too full already is the grave
Of fellows that were good and brave
   And died because they were.

XXXIX

When summer's end is nighing
  And skies at evening cloud,
I muse on change and fortune
  And all the feats I vowed
  When I was young and proud.

The weathercock at sunset
  Would lose the slanted ray,
And I would climb the beacon
  That looked to Wales away
  And saw the last of day.

From hill and cloud and heaven
  The hues of evening died;
Night welled through lane and hollow
  And hushed the countryside,
  But I had youth and pride.

And I with earth and nightfall
  In converse high would stand,
Late, till the west was ashen
  And darkness hard at hand,
  And the eye lost the land.

The year might age, and cloudy
   The lessening day might close,
But air of other summers
   Breathed from beyond the snows,
   And I had hope of those.

They came and were and are not
   And come no more anew;
And all the years and seasons
   That ever can ensue
   Must now be worse and few.

So here's an end of roaming
   On eves when autumn nighs:
The ear too fondly listens
   For summer's parting sighs,
   And then the heart replies.

X L

Tell me not here, it needs not saying,
 What tune the enchantress plays
In aftermaths of soft September
 Or under blanching mays,
For she and I were long acquainted
 And I knew all her ways.

On russet floors, by waters idle,
 The pine lets fall its cone;
The cuckoo shouts all day at nothing
 In leafy dells alone;
And traveller's joy beguiles in autumn
 Hearts that have lost their own.

On acres of the seeded grasses
 The changing burnish heaves;
Or marshalled under moons of harvest
 Stand still all night the sheaves;
Or beeches strip in storms for winter
 And stain the wind with leaves.

Possess, as I possessed a season,
 The countries I resign,
Where over elmy plains the highway
 Would mount the hills and shine,
And full of shade the pillared forest
 Would murmur and be mine.

For nature, heartless, witless nature,
   Will neither care nor know
What stranger's feet may find the meadow
   And trespass there and go,
Nor ask amid the dews of morning
   If they are mine or no.

XLI

FANCY'S KNELL

When lads were home from labour
   At Abdon under Clee,
A man would call his neighbour
   And both would send for me.
And where the light in lances
   Across the mead was laid,
There to the dances
   I fetched my flute and played.

Ours were idle pleasures,
   Yet oh, content we were,
The young to wind the measures,
   The old to heed the air;
And I to lift with playing
   From tree and tower and steep
The light delaying,
   And flute the sun to sleep.

The youth toward his fancy
   Would turn his brow of tan,
And Tom would pair with Nancy
   And Dick step off with Fan;
The girl would lift her glances
   To his, and both be mute:
Well went the dances
   At evening to the flute.

Wenlock Edge was umbered,
   And bright was Abdon Burf,
And warm between them slumbered
   The smooth green miles of turf;
Until from grass and clover
   The upshot beam would fade,
And England over
   Advanced the lofty shade.

The lofty shade advances,
   I fetch my flute and play:
Come, lads, and learn the dances
   And praise the tune to-day.
To-morrow, more's the pity,
   Away we both must hie,
To air the ditty,
   And to earth I.

MORE POEMS

They say my verse is sad: no wonder.
    Its narrow measure spans
Tears of eternity, and sorrow
    Not mine, but man's.

This is for all ill-treated fellows
    Unborn and unbegot,
For them to read when they're in trouble
    And I am not.

I

EASTER HYMN

If in that Syrian garden, ages slain,
You sleep, and know not you are dead in vain,
Nor even in dreams behold how dark and bright
Ascends in smoke and fire by day and night
The hate you died to quench and could but fan,
Sleep well and see no morning, son of man.

But if, the grave rent and the stone rolled by,
At the right hand of majesty on high
You sit, and sitting so remember yet
Your tears, your agony and bloody sweat,
Your cross and passion and the life you gave,
Bow hither out of heaven and see and save.

II

When Israel out of Egypt came
　Safe in the sea they trod;
By day in cloud, by night in flame,
　Went on before them God.

He brought them with a stretched out hand
　Dry-footed through the foam,
Past sword and famine, rock and sand,
　Lust and rebellion, home.

I never over Horeb heard
　The blast of advent blow;
No fire-faced prophet brought me word
　Which way behoved me go.

Ascended is the cloudy flame,
　The mount of thunder dumb;
The tokens that to Israel came,
　To me they have not come.

I see the country far away
　Where I shall never stand;
The heart goes where no footstep may
　Into the promised land.

The realm I look upon and die
    Another man will own;
He shall attain the heaven that I
    Perish and have not known.

But I will go where they are hid
    That never were begot,
To my inheritance amid
    The nation that is not.

When mixed with me the sandstorms drift
    And nerve and thew and brain
Are ashes for the air to lift
    And lightly shower again.

III

For these of old the trader
   Unpearled the Indian seas,
The nations of the nadir
   Were diamondless for these;

A people prone and haggard
   Beheld their lightnings hurled:
All round, like Sinai, staggered
   The sceptre-shaken world.

But now their coins are tarnished,
   Their towers decayed away,
Their kingdom swept and garnished
   For haler kings than they;

Their arms the rust hath eaten,
   Their statutes none regard:
Arabia shall not sweeten
   Their dust, with all her nard.

They cease from long vexation,
   Their nights, their days are done,
The pale, the perished nation
   That never see the sun;

From the old deep-dusted annals
   The years erase their tale,
And round them race the channels
   That take no second sail.

THE SAGE TO THE YOUNG MAN

O youth whose heart is right,
  Whose loins are girt to gain
The hell-defended height
  Where Virtue beckons plain;

Who seest the stark array
  And hast not stayed to count
But singly wilt assay
  The many-cannoned mount:

Well is thy war begun;
  Endure, be strong and strive;
But think not, O my son,
  To save thy soul alive.

Wilt thou be true and just
  And clean and kind and brave?
Well; but for all thou dost
  Be sure it shall not save.

Thou, when the night falls deep,
  Thou, though the mount be won,
High heart, thou shalt but sleep
  The sleep denied to none.

Others, or ever thou,
  To scale those heights were sworn;
And some achieved, but now
  They never see the morn.

How shouldst thou keep the prize?
  Thou wast not born for aye.
Content thee if thine eyes
  Behold it in thy day.

O youth that wilt attain,
  On, for thine hour is short.
It may be thou shalt gain
  The hell-defended fort.

V

DIFFUGERE NIVES

Horace: Odes iv 7

The snows are fled away, leaves on the shaws
    And grasses in the mead renew their birth,
The river to the river-bed withdraws,
    And altered is the fashion of the earth.

The Nymphs and Graces three put off their fear
    And unapparelled in the woodland play.
The swift hour and the brief prime of the year
    Say to the soul, *Thou wast not born for aye.*

Thaw follows frost; hard on the heel of spring
    Treads summer sure to die, for hard on hers
Comes autumn, with his apples scattering;
    Then back to wintertide, when nothing stirs.

But oh, whate'er the sky-led seasons mar,
    Moon upon moon rebuilds it with her beams:
Come *we* where Tullus and where Ancus are,
    And good Aeneas, we are dust and dreams.

Torquatus, if the gods in heaven shall add
    The morrow to the day, what tongue has told?
Feast then thy heart, for what thy heart has had
    The fingers of no heir will ever hold.

When thou descendest once the shades among,
    The stern assize and equal judgment o'er,
Not thy long lineage nor thy golden tongue,
    No, nor thy righteousness, shall friend thee more.

Night holds Hippolytus the pure of stain,
    Diana steads him nothing, he must stay;
And Theseus leaves Pirithoüs in the chain
    The love of comrades cannot take away.

VI

I to my perils
  Of cheat and charmer
  Came clad in armour
By stars benign.
Hope lies to mortals
  And most believe her,
  But man's deceiver
Was never mine.

The thoughts of others
  Were light and fleeting,
  Of lovers' meeting
Or luck or fame.
Mine were of trouble,
  And mine were steady;
  So I was ready
When trouble came.

VII

Stars, I have seen them fall,
   But when they drop and die
No star is lost at all
   From all the star-sown sky.
The toil of all that be
   Helps not the primal fault;
It rains into the sea,
   And still the sea is salt.

VIII

Give me a land of boughs in leaf,
　A land of trees that stand;
Where trees are fallen, there is grief;
　I love no leafless land.

Alas, the country whence I fare,
　It is where I would stay;
And where I would not, it is there
　That I shall be for aye.

And one remembers, and one forgets,
　But 'tis not found again,
Not though they hale in crimsoned nets
　The sunset from the main.

IX

When green buds hang in the elm like dust
   And sprinkle the lime like rain,
Forth I wander, forth I must,
   And drink of life again.
Forth I must by hedgerow bowers
   To look at the leaves uncurled
And stand in the fields where cuckoo-flowers
   Are lying about the world.

X

The weeping Pleiads wester,
 And the moon is under seas;
From bourn to bourn of midnight
 Far sighs the rainy breeze:

It sighs from a lost country
 To a land I have not known;
The weeping Pleiads wester,
 And I lie down alone.

XI

The rainy Pleiads wester,
 Orion plunges prone,
The stroke of midnight ceases,
 And I lie down alone.

The rainy Pleiads wester
 And seek beyond the sea
The head that I shall dream of,
 And 'twill not dream of me.

XII

I promise nothing: friends will part;
　All things may end, for all began;
And truth and singleness of heart
　Are mortal even as is man.

But this unlucky love should last
　When answered passions thin to air;
Eternal fate so deep has cast
　Its sure foundation of despair.

XIII

I lay me down and slumber
  And every morn revive.
Whose is the night-long breathing
  That keeps a man alive?

When I was off to dreamland
  And left my limbs forgot,
Who stayed at home to mind them
  And breathed when I did not?

            .   .   .   .   .

—I waste my time in talking,
  No heed at all takes he,
My kind and foolish comrade
  That breathes all night for me.

XIV

The farms of home lie lost in even,
   I see far off the steeple stand;
West and away from here to heaven
   Still is the land.

There if I go no girl will greet me,
   No comrade hollo from the hill,
No dog run down the yard to meet me:
   The land is still.

The land is still by farm and steeple,
   And still for me the land may stay:
There I was friends with perished people,
   And there lie they.

X V

Tarry, delight; so seldom met,
   So sure to perish, tarry still;
Forbear to cease or languish yet,
   Though soon you must and will.

By Sestos town, in Hero's tower,
   On Hero's heart Leander lies;
The signal torch has burned its hour
   And sputters as it dies.

Beneath him, in the nighted firth,
   Between two continents complain
The seas he swam from earth to earth
   And he must swim again.

XVI

How clear, how lovely bright,
How beautiful to sight
    Those beams of morning play;
How heaven laughs out with glee
Where, like a bird set free,
Up from the eastern sea
    Soars the delightful day.

To-day I shall be strong,
No more shall yield to wrong,
    Shall squander life no more;
Days lost, I know not how,
I shall retrieve them now;
Now I shall keep the vow
    I never kept before.

—Ensanguining the skies
How heavily it dies
    Into the west away;
Past touch and sight and sound,
Not further to be found,
How hopeless under ground
    Falls the remorseful day.

XVII

Bells in tower at evening toll,
And the light forsakes the soul;
Soon will evening's self be gone
And the whispering night come on.

Blame not thou the faulting light
Nor the whispers of the night:
Though the whispering night were still,
Yet the heart would counsel ill.

XVIII

Delight it is in youth and May
  To see the morn arise,
And more delight to look all day
  A lover in the eyes.
Oh maiden, let your distaff be,
And pace the flowery meads with me,
  And I will tell you lies.

'Tis blithe to see the sunshine fail,
  And hear the land grow still
And listen till the nightingale
  Is heard beneath the hill.
Oh follow me where she is flown
Into the leafy woods alone,
  And I will work you ill.

XIX

The mill-stream, now that noises cease,
Is all that does not hold its peace;
Under the bridge it murmurs by,
And here are night and hell and I.

Who made the world I cannot tell;
'Tis made, and here am I in hell.
My hand, though now my knuckles bleed,
I never soiled with such a deed.

And so, no doubt, in time gone by,
Some have suffered more than I,
Who only spend the night alone
And strike my fist upon the stone.

XX

Like mine, the veins of these that slumber
  Leapt once with dancing fires divine;
The blood of all this noteless number
  Ran red like mine.

How still, with every pulse in station,
  Frost in the founts that used to leap,
The put to death, the perished nation,
  How sound they sleep!

These too, these veins which life convulses,
  Wait but a while, shall cease to bound;
I with the ice in all my pulses
  Shall sleep as sound.

XXI

The world goes none the lamer,
   For aught that I can see,
Because this cursed trouble
   Has struck my days and me.

The stars of heaven are steady,
   The founded hills remain,
Though I to earth and darkness
   Return in blood and pain.

Farewell to all belongings
   I won or bought or stole;
Farewell, my lusty carcass,
   Farewell, my aery soul.

Oh worse remains for others
   And worse to fear had I
Than here at four-and-twenty
   To lay me down and die.

X X I I

Ho, everyone that thirsteth
  And hath the price to give,
Come to the stolen waters,
  Drink and your soul shall live.

Come to the stolen waters,
  And leap the guarded pale,
And pull the flower in season
  Before desire shall fail.

It shall not last for ever,
  No more than earth and skies;
But he that drinks in season
  Shall live before he dies.

June suns, you cannot store them
  To warm the winter's cold,
The lad that hopes for heaven
  Shall fill his mouth with mould.

XXIII

Crossing alone the nighted ferry
　　With the one coin for fee,
Whom, on the wharf of Lethe waiting,
　　Count you to find? not me.

The fond lackey to fetch and carry,
　　The true, sick-hearted slave,
Expect him not in the just city
　　And free land of the grave.

XXIV

Stone, steel, dominions pass,
　Faith too, no wonder;
So leave alone the grass
　That I am under.

All knots that lovers tie
　Are tied to sever.
Here shall your sweetheart lie,
　Untrue for ever.

XXV

Yon flakes that fret the eastern sky
   Lead back my day of birth;
The far, wide-wandered hour when I
   Came crying upon earth.

Then came I crying, and to-day,
   With heavier cause to plain,
Depart I into death away,
   Not to be born again.

XXVI

I COUNSEL YOU BEWARE

Good creatures, do you love your lives
  And have you ears for sense?
Here is a knife like other knives,
  That cost me eighteen pence.

I need but stick it in my heart
  And down will come the sky,
And earth's foundations will depart
  And all you folk will die.

XXVII

To stand up straight and tread the turning mill,
To lie flat and know nothing and be still,
   Are the two trades of man; and which is worse
I know not, but I know that both are ill.

XXVIII

He, standing hushed, a pace or two apart,
   Among the bluebells of the listless plain,
Thinks, and remembers how he cleansed his heart
   And washed his hands in innocence in vain.

XXIX

From the wash the laundress sends
My collars home with ravelled ends:
I must fit, now these are frayed,
My neck with new ones, London-made.
Homespun collars, homespun hearts,
Wear to rags in foreign parts.
Mine at least's as good as done,
And I must get a London one.

X X X

Shake hands, we shall never be friends, all's over;
    I only vex you the more I try.
All's wrong that ever I've done or said,
And nought to help it in this dull head:
    Shake hands, here's luck, good-bye.

But if you come to a road where danger
    Or guilt or anguish or shame's to share,
Be good to the lad that loves you true
And the soul that was born to die for you,
    And whistle and I'll be there.

XXXI

Because I liked you better
  Than suits a man to say,
It irked you and I promised
  To throw the thought away.

To put the world between us
  We parted, stiff and dry:
'Good-bye', said you, 'forget me';
  'I will, no fear', said I.

If e'er, where clover whitens
  The dead man's knoll, you pass,
And no tall flower to meet you
  Starts in the trefoiled grass,

Halt by the headstone naming
  The heart you have not stirred,
And say the lad that loved you
  Was one that kept his word.

XXXII

With seed the sowers scatter
    The furrows as they go.
Poor lads, 'tis little matter
    How many sorts they sow,
    For only one will grow.

The charlock on the fallow
    Will take the traveller's eyes,
And gild the ploughland sallow
    With flowers before it dies,
    But twice 'twill not arise.

The stinging-nettle only
    Will still be sure to stand:
The numberless, the lonely,
    The thronger of the land,
    The leaf that hurts the hand.

That thrives, come sun, come showers;
    Blow east, blow west, it springs;
It peoples towns, and towers
    About the courts of Kings,
    And touch it and it stings.

XXXIII

On forelands high in heaven,
  'Tis many a year gone by,
Amidst the fall of even
  Would stand my friends and I.
Before our foolish faces
  Lay lands we did not see;
Our eyes were in the places
  Where we should never be.

'Oh, the pearl seas are yonder,
  The gold and amber shore;
Shires where the girls are fonder,
  Towns where the pots hold more.
And here fust we and moulder
  By grange and rick and shed
And every moon are older,
  And soon we shall be dead.'

Heigho, 'twas true and pity;
  But there we lads must stay.
Troy was a steepled city,
  But Troy was far away.
And home we turned lamenting
  To plains we longed to leave,
And silent hills indenting
  The orange band of eve.

I see the air benighted
    And all the dusking dales,
And lamps in England lighted,
    And evening wrecked on Wales.
And starry darkness paces
    The road from sea to sea,
And blots the foolish faces
    Of my poor friends and me.

XXXIV

Young is the blood that yonder
    Strides out the dusty mile
And breasts the hill-side highway
    And whistles loud the while
    And vaults the stile.

Yet backs, I think, have burdens
    And shoulders carry care:
Even as in other seasons,
    When I and not my heir
    Was young and there.

On miry meads in winter
    The football sprang and fell,
May stuck the land with wickets:
    For all that eye could tell
    The world went well.

Yet well, God knows, it went not,
    God knows, it went awry;
For me, one flowery Maytime,
    It went so ill that I
    Designed to die.

And if so long I carry
    The lot that season marred,
'Tis that the sons of Adam
    Are not so evil-starred
    As they are hard.

Young is the blood that yonder
    Succeeds to rick and fold,
Fresh are the form and favour
    And new the minted mould:
    The thoughts are old.

XXXV

Half-way, for one commandment broken,
   The woman made her endless halt,
And she to-day, a glistering token,
   Stands in the wilderness of salt.
Behind, the vats of judgment brewing
   Thundered, and thick the brimstone snowed:
He to the hill of his undoing
   Pursued his road.

XXXVI

Here dead lie we because we did not choose
  To live and shame the land from which we sprung.
Life, to be sure, is nothing much to lose;
  But young men think it is, and we were young.

XXXVII

I did not lose my heart in summer's even,
    When roses to the moonrise burst apart:
When plumes were under heel and lead was flying,
    In blood and smoke and flame I lost my heart.

I lost it to a soldier and a foeman,
    A chap that did not kill me, but he tried;
That took the sabre straight and took it striking
    And laughed and kissed his hand to me and died.

XXXVIII

By shores and woods and steeples
  Rejoicing hearts receive
Poured on a hundred peoples
  The far-shed alms of eve.

Her hands are filled with slumber
  For world-wide labourers worn;
Yet those are more in number
  That know her not from morn.

Now who sees night for ever,
  He sees no happier sight:
Night and no moon and never
  A star upon the night.

XXXIX

My dreams are of a field afar
  And blood and smoke and shot.
There in their graves my comrades are,
  In my grave I am not.

I too was taught the trade of man
  And spelt the lesson plain;
But they, when I forgot and ran,
  Remembered and remain.

X L

Farewell to a name and a number
   Recalled again
To darkness and silence and slumber
   In blood and pain.

So ceases and turns to the thing
   He was born to be
A soldier cheap to the King
   And dear to me;

So smothers in blood the burning
   And flaming flight
Of valour and truth returning
   To dust and night.

XLI

He looked at me with eyes I thought
    I was not like to find,
The voice he begged for pence with brought
    Another man to mind.

Oh no, lad, never touch your cap;
    It is not my half-crown:
You have it from a better chap
    That long ago lay down.

Turn east and over Thames to Kent
    And come to the sea's brim,
And find his everlasting tent
    And touch your cap to him.

XLII

A. J. J.

When he's returned I'll tell him — oh,
  Dear fellow, I forgot:
Time was you would have cared to know,
  But now it matters not.

I mourn you, and you heed not how;
  Unsaid the word must stay;
Last month was time enough, but now
  The news must keep for aye.

Oh, many a month before I learn
  Will find me starting still
And listening, as the days return,
  For him that never will.

Strange, strange to think his blood is cold
  And mine flows easy on,
And that straight look, that heart of gold,
  That grace, that manhood, gone.

The word unsaid will stay unsaid
  Though there was much to say;
Last month was time enough: he's dead,
  The news must keep for aye.

XLIII

I wake from dreams and turning
    My vision on the height
I scan the beacons burning
    About the fields of night.

Each in its steadfast station
    Inflaming heaven they flare;
They sign with conflagration
    The empty moors of air.

The signal-fires of warning
    They blaze, but none regard;
And on through night to morning
    The world runs ruinward.

XLIV

Far known to sea and shore,
   Foursquare and founded well,
A thousand years it bore,
   And then the belfry fell.
      The steersman of Triest
      Looked where his mark should be,
      But empty was the west
      And Venice under sea.

From dusty wreck dispersed
   Its stature mounts amain;
On surer foot than first
   The belfry stands again.
      At to-fall of the day
      Again its curfew tolls
      And burdens far away
      The green and sanguine shoals.

It looks to north and south,
   It looks to east and west;
It guides to Lido mouth
   The steersman of Triest.
      Andrea, fare you well;
      Venice, farewell to thee.
      The tower that stood and fell
      Is not rebuilt in me.

X·L V

Smooth between sea and land
Is laid the yellow sand,
And here through summer days
Man born of woman plays.

Here the child comes to found
His unremaining mound,
And the grown lad to score
Two names upon the shore.

Here, on the level sand,
Between the sea and land,
What shall I build or write
Against the fall of night?

Tell me of runes to grave
That hold the bursting wave,
Or bastions to design
For longer date than mine.

Shall it be Troy or Rome
I fence against the foam,
Or my own name, to stay
When I depart for aye?

Nothing: too near at hand,
Planing the figured sand,
Effacing clean and fast
Cities not built to last
And words inscribed in vain,
Pours the confounding main.

XLVI

THE LAND OF BISCAY

Hearken, landsmen, hearken, seamen,
    to the tale of grief and me
Looking from the land of Biscay
    on the waters of the sea.

Looking from the land of Biscay
    over Ocean to the sky
On the far-beholding foreland
    paced at even grief and I.
There, as warm the west was burning
    and the east uncoloured cold,
Down the waterway of sunset
    drove to shore a ship of gold.
Gold of mast and gold of cordage,
    gold of sail to sight was she;
And she glassed her ensign golden
    in the waters of the sea.

Oh, said I, my friend and lover,
    take we now that ship and sail
Outward in the ebb of hues and
    steer upon the sunset trail;
Leave the night to fall behind us
    and the clouding countries leave:
Help for you and me is yonder,
    in a haven west of eve.

Under hill she neared the harbour,
    till the gazer could behold
On the golden deck the steersman
    standing at the helm of gold,
Man and ship and sky and water
    burning in a single flame;
And the mariner of Ocean,
    he was calling as he came:
From the highway of the sunset
    he was shouting on the sea,
'Landsman of the land of Biscay,
    have you help for grief and me?'

When I heard I did not answer,
    I stood mute and shook my head:
Son of earth and son of Ocean,
    much we thought and nothing said.
Grief and I abode the nightfall,
    to the sunset grief and he
Turned them from the land of Biscay
    on the waters of the sea.

XLVII

FOR MY FUNERAL

O thou that from thy mansion,
　　Through time and place to roam,
Dost send abroad thy children,
　　And then dost call them home,

That men and tribes and nations
　　And all thy hand hath made
May shelter them from sunshine
　　In thine eternal shade:

We now to peace and darkness
　　And earth and thee restore
Thy creature that thou madest
　　And wilt cast forth no more.

XLVIII

PARTA QUIES

Good-night; ensured release,
Imperishable peace,
    Have these for yours,
While sea abides, and land,
And earth's foundations stand,
    And heaven endures.

When earth's foundations flee,
Nor sky nor land nor sea
    At all is found,
Content you, let them burn:
It is not your concern;
    Sleep on, sleep sound.

ADDITIONAL POEMS

I

ATYS

'Lydians, lords of Hermus river,
　Sifters of the golden loam,
See you yet the lances quiver
　And the hunt returning home?'

'King, the star that shuts the even
　Calls the sheep from Tmolus down;
Home return the doves from heaven,
　And the prince to Sardis town.'

From the hunting heavy laden
　Up the Mysian road they ride;
And the star that mates the maiden
　Leads his son to Croesus' side.

'Lydians, under stream and fountain
　Finders of the golden vein,
Riding from Olympus mountain,
　Lydians, see you Atys plain?'

'King, I see the Phrygian stranger
　And the guards in hunter's trim,
Saviours of thy son from danger;
　Them I see. I see not him.'

'Lydians, as the troop advances,
   — It is eve and I am old —
Tell me why they trail their lances,
   Washers of the sands of gold.

'I am old and day is ending
   And the wildering night comes on;
Up the Mysian entry wending,
   Lydians, Lydians, what is yon?'

Hounds behind their master whining,
   Huntsmen pacing dumb beside,
On his breast the boar-spear shining,
   Home they bear his father's pride.

II

Oh were he and I together,
    Shipmates on the fleeted main,
Sailing through the summer weather
    To the spoil of France or Spain.

Oh were he and I together,
    Locking hands and taking leave,
Low upon the trampled heather
    In the battle lost at eve.

Now are he and I asunder
    And asunder to remain;
Kingdoms are for others' plunder,
    And content for other slain.

III

When Adam walked in Eden young
   Happy, 'tis writ, was he,
While high the fruit of knowledge hung
   Unbitten on the tree.

Happy was he the livelong day:
   I doubt 'tis written wrong.
The heart of man, for all they say,
   Was never happy long.

And now my feet are tired of rest
   And here they will not stay
And the soul fevers in my breast
   And aches to be away.

IV

It is no gift I tender,
  A loan is all I can;
But do not scorn the lender;
  Man gets no more from man.

Oh, mortal man may borrow
  What mortal man can lend;
And 'twill not end to-morrow,
  Though sure enough 'twill end.

If death and time are stronger,
  A love may yet be strong;
The world will last for longer,
  But this will last for long.

V

Here are the skies, the planets seven,
And all the starry train:
Content you with the mimic heaven,
And on the earth remain.[1]

[1] Written by A. E. H. on the flyleaf of a copy of *Manilius,*
Book I, which he gave to Walter Headlam.

V I

Ask me no more, for fear I should reply;
　Others have held their tongues, and so can I;
Hundreds have died, and told no tale before:
　Ask me no more, for fear I should reply —

How one was true and one was clean of stain
　And one was braver than the heavens are high,
And one was fond of me: and all are slain.
　Ask me no more, for fear I should reply.

VII

He would not stay for me; and who can wonder?
He would not stay for me to stand and gaze.
I shook his hand and tore my heart in sunder
And went with half my life about my ways.

VIII

Now to her lap the incestuous earth
   The son she bore has ta'en,
And other sons she brings to birth
   But not my friend again.

I X

When the bells justle in the tower
   The hollow night amid,
Then on my tongue the taste is sour
   Of all I ever did.

X

Oh, on my breast in days hereafter
  Light the earth should lie,
Such weight to bear is now the air,
  So heavy hangs the sky.

XI

GOD'S ACRE

Morning up the eastern stair
Marches, azuring the air,
And the foot of twilight still
Is stolen toward the western sill.
Blithe the maids go milking, blithe
Men in hayfields stone the scythe;
All the land's alive around
Except the churchyard's idle ground.
There's empty acres west and east,
But aye 'tis God's that bears the least:
This hopeless garden that they sow
With the seeds that never grow.
They shall have breath that never were,
But he that was shall have it ne'er;
The unconceived and unbegot
Shall look on heaven, but he shall not.
The heart with many wildfires lit,
Ice is not so cold as it.
The thirst that rivers could not lay
A little dust has quenched for aye;
And in a fathom's compass lie
Thoughts much wider than the sky.

XII

AN EPITAPH

Stay, if you list, O passer by the way;
Yet night approaches: better not to stay.
   I never sigh, nor flush, nor knit the brow,
   Nor grieve to think how ill God made me, now.
Here, with one balm for many fevers found,
Whole of an ancient evil, I sleep sound.

XIII

Oh turn not in from marching
   To taverns on the way.
The drought and thirst and parching
   A little dust will lay,
   And take desire away.

Oh waste no words a-wooing
   The soft sleep to your bed;
She is not worth pursuing,
   You will so soon be dead;
   And death will serve instead.

XIV

'Oh is it the jar of nations,
　The noise of a world run mad,
The fleeing of earth's foundations?'
　Yes, yes; lie quiet, my lad.

'Oh is it my country calling,
　And whom will my country find
To shore up the sky from falling?'
　My business; never you mind.

'Oh is it the newsboys crying
　Lost battle, retreat, despair,
And honour and England dying?'
　Well, fighting-cock, what if it were?

The devil this side of the darnels
　Is having a dance with man,
And quarrelsome chaps in charnels
　Must bear it as best they can.

XV

'Tis five years since, 'An end', said I,
'I'll march no further, time to die.
All's lost; no worse has heaven to give.'
Worse it has given, and yet I live.

I shall not die to-day, no fear:
I shall live yet for many a year,
And see worse ills and worse again,
And die of age and not of pain.

When God would rear from earth aloof
The blue height of the hollow roof,
He sought him pillars sure and strong
And ere he found them sought them long.

The stark steel splintered from the thrust,
The basalt mountain sprang to dust,
The blazing pier of diamond flawed
In shards of rainbows all abroad.

What found he, that the heavens stand fast?
What pillar proven firm at last
Bears up so light that world-seen span?
The heart of man, the heart of man.

XVI

Some can gaze and not be sick
But I could never learn the trick.
There's this to say for blood and breath,
They give a man a taste for death.

XVII

The stars have not dealt me the worst they could do:
My pleasures are plenty, my troubles are two.
But oh, my two troubles they reave me of rest,
The brains in my head and the heart in my breast.

Oh, grant me the ease that is granted so free,
The birthright of multitudes, give it to me,
That relish their victuals and rest on their bed
With flint in the bosom and guts in the head.

XVIII

Oh who is that young sinner with the handcuffs on his wrists?
And what has he been after that they groan and shake their
  fists?
And wherefore is he wearing such a conscience-stricken air?
Oh they're taking him to prison for the colour of his hair.

'Tis a shame to human nature, such a head of hair as his;
In the good old time 'twas hanging for the colour that it is;
Though hanging isn't bad enough and flaying would be fair
For the nameless and abominable colour of his hair.

Oh a deal of pains he's taken and a pretty price he's paid
To hide his poll or dye it of a mentionable shade;
But they've pulled the beggar's hat off for the world to see and
  stare,
And they're haling him to justice for the colour of his hair.

Now 'tis oakum for his fingers and the treadmill for his feet
And the quarry-gang on Portland in the cold and in the heat,
And between his spells of labour in the time he has to spare
He can curse the God that made him for the colour of his hair.

XIX

THE DEFEATED

In battles of no renown
My fellows and I fell down,
And over the dead men roar
The battles they lost before.

The thunderstruck flagstaffs fall,
The earthquake breaches the wall,
The far-felled steeples resound,
And we lie under the ground.

O soldiers, saluted afar
By them that had seen your star,
In conquest and freedom and pride
Remember your friends that died.

Amid rejoicing and song
Remember, my lads, how long,
How deep the innocent trod
The grapes of the anger of God.

XX

I shall not die for you,
　　Another fellow may;
Good lads are left and true
　　Though one departs away.
　　But he departs to-day
And leaves his work to do,
　　For I was luckless aye
And shall not die for you.

XXI

NEW YEAR'S EVE

The end of the year fell chilly
    Between a moon and a moon;
Thorough the twilight shrilly
    The bells rang, ringing no tune.

The windows stained with story,
    The walls with miracle scored,
Were hidden for gloom and glory
    Filling the house of the Lord.

Arch and aisle and rafter
    And roof-tree dizzily high
Were full of weeping and laughter
    And song and saying good-bye.

There stood in the holy places
    A multitude none could name,
Ranks of dreadful faces
    Flaming, transfigured in flame.

Crown and tiar and mitre
    Were starry with gold and gem;
Christmas never was whiter
    Than fear on the face of them.

In aisles that emperors vaulted
    For a faith the world confessed,
Abasing the Host exalted,
    They worshipped towards the west.

They brought with laughter oblation;
    They prayed, not bowing the head;
They made without tear lamentation,
    And rendered me answer and said:

'Oh thou that seest our sorrow,
    It fares with us even thus:
To-day we are gods, to-morrow
    Hell have mercy on us.

'Lo, morning over our border
    From out of the west comes cold;
Down ruins the ancient order
    And empire builded of old.

'Our house at even is queenly
    With psalm and censers alight:
Look thou never so keenly
    Thou shalt not find us to-night.

'We are come to the end appointed
    With sands not many to run;
Divinities disanointed
    And kings whose kingdom is done.

'The peoples knelt down at our portal,
    All kindreds under the sky;
We were gods and implored and immortal
    Once; and to-day we die.'

They turned them again to their praying,
    They worshipped and took no rest,
Singing old tunes and saying
    'We have seen his star in the west',

Old tunes of the sacred psalters,
    Set to wild farewells;
And I left them there at their altars
    Ringing their own dead knells.

XXII

R. L. S.

Home is the sailor, home from sea:
    Her far-borne canvas furled,
The ship pours shining on the quay
    The plunder of the world.

Home is the hunter from the hill:
    Fast in the boundless snare
All flesh lies taken at his will
    And every fowl of air.

'Tis evening on the moorland free,
    The starlit wave is still:
Home is the sailor from the sea,
    The hunter from the hill.

XXIII

THE OLIVE

The olive in its orchard
   Should now be rooted sure,
To cast abroad its branches
   And flourish and endure.

Aloft amid the trenches
   Its dressers dug and died
The olive in its orchard
   Should prosper and abide.

Close should the fruit be clustered
   And light the leaf should wave,
So deep the root is planted
   In the corrupting grave.

TRANSLATIONS

Aeschylus, *Septem Contra Thebas* (lines 848-860)

Now do our eyes behold
The tidings which were told:
Twin fallen kings, twin perished hopes to mourn,
   The slayer, the slain,
The entangled doom forlorn
   And ruinous end of twain.
Say, is not sorrow, is not sorrow's sum
On home and hearthstone come?
   O waft with sighs the sail from shore,
O smite the bosom, cadencing the oar
That rows beyond the rueful stream for aye
     To the far strand,
   The ship of souls, the dark,
   The unreturning bark
Whereon light never falls nor foot of Day,
Ev'n to the bourne of all, to the unbeholden land.

Sophocles, *Oedipus Coloneus* (lines 1211-1248)

What man is he that yearneth
    For length unmeasured of days?
Folly mine eye discerneth
    Encompassing all his ways.
For years over-running the measure
    Shall change thee in evil wise:
Grief draweth nigh thee; and pleasure,
    Behold, it is hid from thine eyes.
    This to their wage have they
    Which overlive their day.
And He that looseth from labour
    Doth one with other befriend,
    Whom bride nor bridesmen attend,
Song, nor sound of the tabor,
    Death, that maketh an end.

Thy portion esteem I highest,
    Who wast not ever begot;
Thine next, being born who diest
    And straightway again art not.
With follies light as the feather
    Doth Youth to man befall;
Then evils gather together,
    There wants not one of them all —
    Wrath, envy, discord, strife,
    The sword that seeketh life.

And sealing the sum of trouble
   Doth tottering Age draw nigh,
   Whom friends and kinsfolk fly,
Age, upon whom redouble
   All sorrows under the sky.

This man, as me, even so,
Have the evil days overtaken;
And like as a cape sea-shaken
With tempest at earth's last verges
And shock of all winds that blow,
His head the seas of woe,
The thunders of awful surges
Ruining overflow;
Blown from the fall of even,
   Blown from the dayspring forth,
Blown from the noon in heaven,
   Blown from night and the North.

Euripides, *Alcestis* (lines 962-1005)

In heaven-high musings and many,
   Far seeking and deep debate,
Of strong things find I not any
   That is as the strength of Fate.
Help nor healing is told
In soothsayings uttered of old,
In the Thracian runes, the verses
   Engraven of Orpheus' pen;
No balm of virtue to save
Apollo aforetime gave,
Who stayeth with tender mercies
   The plagues of the children of men.

She hath not her habitation
   In temples that hands have wrought;
Him that bringeth oblation,
   Behold, she heedeth him naught.
Be thou not wroth with us more,
O mistress, than heretofore;
For what God willeth soever,
   That thou bringest to be;
Thou breakest in sunder the brand
Far forged in the Iron Land;
Thine heart is cruel, and never
   Came pity anigh unto thee.

Thee too, O King, hath she taken
   And bound in her tenfold chain;
   Yet faint not, neither complain:
The dead thou wilt not awaken
   For all thy weeping again.
They perish, whom gods begot;
The night releaseth them not.
Beloved was she that died
And dear shall ever abide,
For this was the queen among women, Admetus, that lay
   by thy side.

Not as the multitude lowly
   Asleep in their sepulchres,
   Not as their grave be hers,
But like as the gods held holy,
   The worship of wayfarers.
Yea, all that travel the way
Far off shall see it and say,
Lo, erst for her lord she died,
To-day she sitteth enskied;
Hail, lady, be gracious to usward; that alway her honour
   abide.

HISTORY OF THE TEXT

The main events in the textual history of *A Shropshire Lad* (London: Kegan Paul, Trench, Trübner & Co., 1896) and *Last Poems* (London: Grant Richards, 1922) may here be summed up briefly, since these two volumes, published in their author's lifetime, underwent a small number of authorized changes. Housman's first publisher having declined to reissue *A Shropshire Lad,* the second edition was brought out by Grant Richards in 1898. The type for this printing was reset and, in its composition, several unwarranted changes in the text (the author did not see the proof sheets) were introduced: thirty-three in punctuation, six in spelling, and four other minor variations. Most of these innovations seem to have been in the nature of editorial aids to "easier reading" and were not carried into later impressions.

In 1922, Housman made two changes in the text of his first volume: *Loose* replaced *Thick* at the head of line ten of poem number 38; and line nine of number 52, which had read *He hears: long since forgotten,* was altered to *He hears: no more remembered.* Housman gave directions for these two substitutions in the midst of final arrangements for the launching of his second volume of poetry and, reflecting perhaps on the many textual blunders that had disfigured the several printings of *A Shropshire Lad,* remarked hopefully in his Preface to *Last Poems,* ". . . it is best that what I have written should be printed while I am here to see it through the press and control its spelling and punctuation." But his anticipations of textual accuracy were defeated as he turned the pages of his author's

249

copy. He was a passionate and lifelong crusader for typographical perfection and his abundant correspondence with Grant Richards is replete with allusions to faults in the reprintings of his two volumes in England and America.

The only change the author made in *Last Poems* was the addition of a title to the thirty-sixth lyric. Asked by the Headmaster of Winchester College for his permission to include the poem in a school anthology, Housman granted it and added for good measure the new title, "Revolution," which two years later appeared in the seventh printing of his book (1928).

The history of the texts of the two posthumously issued sections of Housman's poetry, *More Poems* and *Additional Poems,* derives mainly from the history after his death, in 1936, of the four notebooks in which, from about 1887 to 1925, he composed and copied practically all the poems in the four sections here under review. By the terms of his will (dated 19 November, 1932), all his books and manuscripts passed into the care of his brother, Laurence Housman, who was permitted to publish, under two conditions, poems which A. E. H. had passed over in collecting the substance of the two volumes described above. These two conditions were that the manuscript poems be completed and up to the average of what he himself had published. The will further directed that, after the new selections had been made, all the remaining drafts of unpublished material must be destroyed.

Laurence Housman chose forty-nine pieces for the volume *More Poems,* which was issued on 26 October, 1936, the London (Cape) and New York (Knopf) editions appearing on the same day. The texts of these two volumes exhibited many variations: thirteen in wording, forty in punctuation, ten in spelling, besides other minor incongruities. When this segment of Housman's poetry passed into the comprehensive edition, THE COL-

LECTED POEMS OF A. E. HOUSMAN (London: Cape, 1939; New York: Holt, 1940), some sixty new variations appeared in the London printing of this book. Thus, in the all-important first issues of the posthumous poetry, a large number of textual faults were sown, some of them, because of the destruction soon to fall upon parts of the Notebooks, now beyond eradication.

Two years prior to the appearance of the comprehensive Cape edition, that company had published Laurence Housman's *A. E. H.,* a memoir of his brother, in which were included eighteen of the twenty-three pieces eventually collected under the title, *Additional Poems.* In the note prefixed to the lyrics in the memoir, there is a comment on the first poem, "Atys," which gives a hint of the textual insecurity underlying much of the material which Laurence was handling, for the basis of "Atys" was a "very rough draft, difficult to reconstruct," a manuscript that the editor confesses would have been of little value without the help of a fair copy seen thirty years before. The rough draft of the poem, in Notebook B, pages 223–224, has not survived. Destroyed with it were large sections of notebook material containing drafts of lyrics printed in *Additional Poems:* the unique holographs of *AP* 2, 6, and 7 and parts of *AP* 4, 11, and 14.

At the same time, it should be said that by far the larger portion of the notebook drafts of *Additional Poems*—and *More Poems* as well—has survived, and with them, seventeen sheets of printer's copy containing pieces once intended for *A Shropshire Lad* and *Last Poems,* all but six uncollected before their appearance among the posthumous poetry. These documents fortunately provide the means by which a substantial number of the errors in the texts published by Housman's first editors can be detected and replaced by their original readings.

In order to explain the survival of these drafts and other proscribed manuscripts, it is necessary to sketch the history of the Notebooks from 1936 to the present. Having taken from them the pieces he wished to publish, Laurence did not sacrifice the entire remainder of unused writing as he had been enjoined to do. He, of necessity, destroyed about 140 sheets that, presumably, contained nothing but interdicted matter and laid aside the rest to be prepared for shipment to America. These included about sixty sheets that contained nothing but drafts of poems that were already, or soon would be, a part of the Housman canon. These were preserved intact. Remaining were about 140 sheets bearing on the recto or the verso, or both, drafts that could be legitimately preserved, alternating with workshop sketching and other poems Laurence had not chosen and consequently should not allow to survive. In the disposition of this material, he took a middle course. After a lengthy process of erasure and cutting, in which some sheets were reduced to small fragments containing only a quatrain, he collected all the cut and uncut leaves and affixed them to mounting sheets, leaving exposed only manuscripts not under the ban; pages and sections containing new or variorum writing survived only at the cost of being subjected to a coat of adhesive and being securely attached to the mounts. When at last these newly mounted *reliquiae* were reassembled and, with a small quantity of other holographs (including the foolscap sheets of printer's copy already mentioned) gathered from sources outside the Notebooks, made into seven new "books," the substance of the four Notebooks had been heavily reduced and the original order of their contents overthrown.

The collection was received by the Library of Congress in 1940. Five years later, upon the advice of a Library consultant, all of the attached sheets and fragments were removed from their mounts, cleaned, and laid inside transparent envelopes; and each piece was reset, hinged on its original mount and in its original position. In its present form, the collection now exhibits, in drafts of varying reliability, holographs of all but twenty of the 177 pieces in the COLLECTED POEMS and, in addition to these, 136 new portions of manuscript that were hidden from view on the glued down pages when the notebook remains were sent to America.

As soon as the full resources of the Washington manuscripts were discovered and reported in the Library bulletins, they attracted much attention, for they are by far the most valuable of the poet's surviving documents and virtually our only reference in matters concerning the texts of the poetry that appeared after his death. However, it must be said that, valuable as they are, the notebook remains in their present condition do not yield their treasure easily. A large number of the drafts, because of cancel marks and erasure and the progressive deterioration resulting from the effects of the adhesive, are very difficult to read; further, the disarray of the manuscripts, being the same as the confused assembly in which Laurence left them, requires that they be used with great care. Before any systematic study of the texts can be undertaken, the four Notebooks must be reconstituted in their original form—as nearly as this can be done by the use of a complete set of photocopies of the sheets and fragments displayed in Volumes II, III, IV, V, VII, and VIII in the Library of Congress collection. Then the proper interrelationships of their 244 pieces can be studied and some sound conclusions can be reached; first and latest drafts of a given poem can be identified and compared, the value of alternative readings estimated, and the quantity of missing manuscript summed up, often within very narrow limits.

It is, then, to such a simulacre of A. E. Housman's original Notebooks that practically all questions pertaining to the texts of *More Poems* and *Additional Poems* must be taken, the exceptions being a small number of poems apparently never entered in the Notebooks and another minor group whose holographs perished by erasure or with dissected portions of sheets that were cut in the process of salvage. It is because of these lacunae that the texts of nine poems must be accepted blindly as they stand in the New York or London edition, but for five of these printed versions exist in periodicals and elsewhere, some of them authorized by the poet himself. Furthermore, the seventeen foolscap sheets, bearing his printer's copy, provide unquestionable authority for collation with the notebook drafts of *MP* 1, 4, 12, 18, 26, 33, 46, and *AP* 18.

There is evidence in the first printings of the posthumous poetry that their editor was responsive to both the restraints and the supports of the notebook drafts, for Laurence Housman provided alternative readings for parts of *MP* 17 and 34 when they appeared in the separate Knopf edition of 1936; he did the same for *AP* 6 and 9 when the eighteen new lyrics were incorporated into his memoir, issued by Cape the following year. This recognition of valid alternatives was not, however, expanded and carried into the comprehensive Cape edition; on the contrary, the four apologetic notes were silently dropped as the editors (or editor) from this time forward assumed the function of arbitrating alternatives left open by the poet in his notebook drafts and fair copies. Even if this arbitration had been permitted by his testamentary instructions, which were precisely to the contrary, it would have been an exceedingly dubious practice, for there is nothing in the record of Housman's handling of the drafts he reworked to produce *A Shropshire Lad* and *Last Poems* to indicate any principle of selection that his editors-to-be might follow when confronted with a line bearing an original and a superscribed reading, both uncanceled. In the notebook drafts of these 105 poems, open alternatives may still be read in seventy-four places: of twenty-one of these, Housman sent his original reading into print; of thirty-seven others, he preferred his second reading; and of sixteen others, he abandoned both readings for a third that went into printer's copy or corrected proofsheets. *Caveat editor.*

It is not within the scope of this CENTENNIAL EDITION to provide a description of the editorial treatment of the many open alternatives and other cruxes in the notebook drafts from which *More Poems* and *Additional Poems* were taken and published; this clarification is possible only on the larger canvas of a full variorum. Nor has it been thought necessary to trace the variations in the text and editorial matter through the fifteen impressions of the London editions since 1939. These fluctuations, some of which brought new errors into the texts, had no influence upon the authorized New York edition, of which the first printing was practically identical with that of the COLLECTED POEMS first issued by Cape and has since 1940 not been altered except for a few corrections not indicated by the Notebooks: *e.g.,* the restoration of a quotation mark chipped from the plate for page 10 and the removal of a hyphen in *far-seeking,* on page 246, a superfluity copied from an anthology and corrected by the poet a few years before his death.

History of the Text

The principal aim, in brief, of the CENTENNIAL EDITION is to present the texts of *A Shropshire Lad* and *Last Poems* essentially as they were in the 1940 New York edition; and the texts of *More Poems* and *Additional Poems* with all necessary corrections derived from a study of the Washington manuscripts begun by the editor over ten years ago.

Columbus, Ohio   TOM BURNS HABER
January, 1959

CHRONOLOGY OF THE POEMS[1]

The analysis of the Notebooks published in Laurence Housman's memoir of his brother (pp. 256–72) includes twenty-seven dated entries, of which four have not survived. Among the others, consisting of fragments and full sheets, are represented sixteen *Shropshire Lad* pieces, four from *Last Poems,* one from *More Poems,* two from *Additional Poems.*

Another valuable source for the chronology of A. E. Housman's poetry is a list of thirty-nine dated titles published by Sir Sydney Cockerell in the *London Times Literary Supplement* for 7 November, 1936 (p. 908). This information was dictated to him by the poet 28 October, 1922, a few days after the publication of *Last Poems.*

T. B. H.

A Shropshire Lad

Once in the wind of morning	Sept. 1890
In summertime on Bredon (first draft)	July 1891
Far in a western brookland	1891–2
'Tis time, I think, by Wenlock town	Feb. 1893
With rue my heart is laden	Aug. 1893 [2]
Farewell to barn and stack and tree	Aug. 1894
The lad came to the door at night (first draft)	Dec. 1894
When I was one-and-twenty (first draft) [3]	Jan. 1895

[1] The publishers are indebted to Messrs. Charles Scribner's Sons for permission to reprint this Chronology from *My Brother, A. E. Housman,* by Laurence Housman. It incorporates the data from both sources mentioned above.

[2] The memoir locates this poem and the date on A 155–7. These pages have survived, complete, but show no trace of the entry.

[3] Only the first line was written, dated, on A 216.

A Shropshire Lad—continued

High the vanes of Shrewsbury gleam	Jan. 1895
Wake: the silver dusk returning (first draft)	Jan. 1895
Leave your home behind, lad	Jan. 1895
On moonlit heath and lonesome bank (first draft)	Feb. 1895
'Far I hear the bugle blow	Mar. 1895
'Tis spring; come out to ramble	Apr. 1895
Oh, when I was in love with you	May 1895
Along the field as we came by	June (1895?) [4]
When I came last to Ludlow	July 1895
Here the hangman stops his cart	Aug. 1895
On Wenlock Edge the wood's in trouble (first draft) [5]	Nov. 1895
In my own shire, if I was sad	Nov. 1895 [6]

Last Poems

Her strong enchantments failing	1895 [7]
Yonder see the morning blink	Dec. 1895
In the morning, in the morning	1895
In midnights of November	Begun 1895, finished *c.* 1905 [8]

[4] The notebook page B 36 that contained this poem is missing. The memoir gives the date June —; 1895 is correct.

[5] This draft was destroyed with page B 97; the following page bears the second draft, lightly corrected.

[6] The only notebook entry of this poem (on B 109–110) was destroyed.

[7] The first draft (page B 76) was written in August or September, 1895, but the memoir has it that A 205 (the lower half of which is missing), written between August and December, 1894, bore five lines of the poem.

[8] The first entry (four or five stanzas) is on A 209, written between August and December, 1894; the second entry (page B 95) is dated October, 1895; fair copy (page D 84–5) was probably written in April, 1922.

Last Poems—continued

The chestnut casts his flambeaux Feb. 1896: [9]	
	last verse, April 1922
Oh hard is the bed they have made him	Before 1899
The laws of God, the laws of man	*c.* 1900 [10]
As I gird on for fighting	*c.* 1900 [11]
When the eye of day is shut	Aug. 1900
The fairies break their dances	*c.* 1900–1905 [12]
Could man be drunk for ever	*c.* 1900–1905
Star and coronal and bell	1900–1922
He is here, Urania's son Begun 1900,[13] finished Apr. 1922	
The sigh that heaves the grasses	Soon after 1900
I 'listed at home for a lancer	Time of Boer War
The Queen she sent to look for me	Time of Boer War
The rain, it streams on stone and hillock	*c.* 1902–1922
Oh stay at home, my lad, and plough	After Boer War
'Tis mute, the word they went to hear	*c.* 1903 [14]
The Wain upon the northern steep	Before 1904
Beyond the moor and mountain crest	*c.* 1905
Soldier from the wars returning	Chiefly 1905
The orchards half the way	*c.* 1905
Onward led the road again	1905–Apr. 1922

[9] The memoir locates fragments of this poem on B 111–12 (destroyed), which must date from the closing weeks of 1895.

[10] First draft on A 201, between August and December, 1894.

[11] Unique draft on B 6–7, April or May, 1895.

[12] The first quatrain was written on A 125 between September, 1890 and July, 1891.

[13] A 216 contains six lines of this poem written December, 1894 or January, 1895.

[14] A. E. H. gave date *c.* 1904; but this poem appeared in *The Venture* in 1903. (This note was added in the memoir.)

Last Poems—continued

'What sound awakened me, I wonder	Begun 1905, finished Apr. 1922
When first my way to fair I took	Before 1910
The night my father got me	Before 1910
I walked alone and thinking	1910–1922
When I would muse in boyhood	After 1910
When summer's end is nighing	1920–1922
He stood, and heard the steeple	1921
West and away	First stanza, 1922, others earlier
Wake not for the world-heard thunder	30 Mar., 1922
We'll to the woods no more	Apr. 1922 [15]
In valleys green and still (except for last verse, written long previously) [16]	Apr. 1922
The night is freezing fast	Apr. 1922
The sloe was lost in flower	Finished Apr. 1922
The half-moon westers low, my love	Apr. 1922
Tell me not here, it needs not saying	Apr. 1922

More Poems

The weeping Pleiads wester	Feb. 1893
O thou that from thy mansion	Jan. 1925

Additional Poems

It is no gift I tender	June 1895
Morning up the eastern stair	Sept. 1895

[15] The memoir describes C 89 as containing "a rough draft of first four lines" of this prologue poem written apparently not many years after 1900.

[16] On B 12, April or May, 1895.

INDEX OF FIRST LINES AND TITLES

Index of First Lines and Titles

Index of First Lines and Titles

Index of First Lines and Titles

266

Index of First Lines and Titles